Language Art

Teacher's Guide

CONTENTS

Revision Editor: Alan Christopherson, M.S.

Alpha Omega Publications®

804 N. 2nd Ave. E., Rock Rapids, IA 51246-1759
© MM by Alpha Omega Publications, Inc.   All rights reserved.
LIFEPAC is a registered trademark of Alpha Omega Publications, Inc.

OVERVIEW

LANGUAGE ARTS

Curriculum Overview
Grades K–12

Kindergarten

Language Arts Lessons

1-40	41-80	81-120	121-160
Alphabet-say the alphabet **Colors-**recognize colors **Directions-**left to right **Following directions-**given once **Grammar-**form simple sentences **Listening skills** **Personal recognition-**read and write first name -know age and address -recognize names of family members **Phonics-**short *a, e, i* vowels -initial: *b, t, m, r, s, n, d, p, l* -form and read simple words -form rhyming words **Shapes-**circle, square, triangle, and rectangle -recognize shapes in objects **Stories and Poems-**create simple stories and poems **Writing-**form circle and lines -*Aa, Bb, Dd, Ee, Ii, Ll, Mm, Nn, Pp, Rr, Ss, and Tt*	**Grammar-**sentences begin with capital, end with period **Patterns-**simple shape, color patterns **Personal recognition-**read and write first and last name **Phonics-**short *a, e, i, o, and u* vowels -initial: *k, c, ck, f, h, g, j, v, w, y, z, qu, and x* -read simple sentences **Position/direction concepts-**in/out, in front of/behind, up/down, on/off, open/closed, over/under **Sequencing-**alphabetical order -simple story **Shapes-**oval **Size concepts-**big/little, large/small **Writing-***Kk, Cc, Ff, Hh, Oo, Gg, Jj, Vv, Ww, Uu, Yy, Zz, Qq, and Xx*	**Phonics-**recognize the short vowel sounds -recognize all initial consonant sounds -recognize long *a, e, i, o,* and *u* sounds -silent *e* -initial consonant digraphs: *sh, ch,* both soft and hard *th* -final consonant sounds: *_b, _ck, _k, _l* **Word recognition-**color words, number words & shape words **Writing-**name -complete alphabet, capital and small letters -all color words -number words: *one, two, three, four, five, six* -shape words: *circle, square, triangle*	**Phonics-**recognize the long vowel sounds -initial consonant diagraphs: *wh;* review *ch, sh, th* -recognize all final consonant sounds: **Stories and poems-**create, tell, and recite stories and poems **Word recognition-**position/direction words: *up/down, high/low, in, inside, out, outside, top/bottom* -number words: *seven, eight, nine, ten* -shape words: *rectangle, oval, star* **Writing-**number words: *seven, eight, nine, ten* -shape words: *rectangle, oval, star* -position/direction words: *up/down, high/low, in, inside, out, outside, top/bottom*

Language Arts LIFEPAC Overview

	Grade 1	Grade 2	Grade 3
LIFEPAC 1	**FUN WITH PHONICS** • Short vowel sounds • Consonants • Main ideas • Rhyming words	**KNOW YOUR NOUNS** • Review vowels & consonants • Beginning, middle, ending sounds • Singular & plural nouns • Common & proper nouns	**OLD AND NEW SKILLS** • Vowels • Consonants • Sentence phrases • Capital letters • Reading skills
LIFEPAC 2	**FUN WITH PHONICS** • Kinds of sentences • Cardinal & ordinal numbers • Suffixes • Plurals • Classifying	**ACTION VERBS** • Vowel digraphs • Action words – verbs • Following directions • The dictionary • ABC order	**BUILDING WORDS • SENTENCES** • Vowels – long, short • Questions • ABC order • Capital letters
LIFEPAC 3	**FUN WITH PHONICS** • Consonant digraphs • Compounds • Syllables • Possessives • Contractions • Soft c and g	**SIMPLE SENTENCES** • r-controlled vowels • Consonant blends • Using capital letters • Subjects & verbs in sentences	**WORDS • GETTING TO THE ROOTS** • Root words • Dictionary guide words • Synonyms • Antonyms • Capital letters
LIFEPAC 4	**FUN WITH PHONICS** • Paragraphs • Silent letters • Sequencing • Subject-verb agreement	**TYPES OF SENTENCES** • Consonant digraphs • Statement, question, exclamation sentences • Using capital letters • The library	**WORDS • HOW TO USE THEM** • Noun • Verb • Adjective • Adverb • Irregular vowels • Composition
LIFEPAC 5	**FUN WITH PHONICS** • Long vowels • Homonyms • Poetry • Syllables • Possessives • Contractions • Plurals • Suffixes	**USING PUNCTUATION** • Diphthongs • Punctuation review • Using a comma • Rules for making words plural • Writing a biography • Contractions	**SENTENCE • START TO FINISH** • Question marks • Commas • Periods • Paragraphs • Plural words
LIFEPAC 6	**FUN WITH PHONICS** • R-controlled vowels • Writing stories • Pronouns • Following directions	**ADJECTIVES** • Rhyming words • Biblical poetry • Adjectives in sentences • Synonyms, antonyms • Thesaurus • Comparative, superlative adjectives	**ALL ABOUT BOOKS** • Books • Stories • Poems • Card catalog • Critical thinking
LIFEPAC 7	**FUN WITH PHONICS** • Vowel digraphs • Letters - business, friendly, invitations • Syllables	**POSSESSIVE NOUNS** • Introduction to letter writing • Pronunciation key • Possessive nouns • Silent consonants • Homonyms	**READING AND WRITING** • For directions • Friendly letters • Pronouns • Fact • Fiction
LIFEPAC 8	**FUN WITH PHONICS** • Vowel digraphs • Subject-verb agreement • Compounds • Contractions • Possessives • Pronouns	**PRONOUNS** • Author's intent & use of titles • Predicting content • Suffixes • Character, setting, & plot • Analogies • Writing in cursive	**READING SKILLS** • For sequence • For detail • Verbs - being, compound • Drama
LIFEPAC 9	**FUN WITH PHONICS** • Vowel digraphs • Titles • Main ideas • Sentences • Paragraphs • Proper nouns	**VERB TYPES AND TENSES** • Review action verbs • Dividing words into syllables • State of being verbs • Past & present verb tenses	**MORE READING & WRITING** • For information • Thank you letters • Book reports • Reference books
LIFEPAC 10	**LOOKING BACK** • Letters and sounds • Contractions • Plurals • Possessives • Sentences • Stories	**LOOKING BACK** • Nouns & verbs • Word division • Consonant blends, digraphs • Prefixes, suffixes, root words • Possessives • Pronouns, adjectives	**LOOKING BACK** • Reading for comprehension • Sentence punctuation • Writing letters • Parts of Speech

Grade 4	Grade 5	Grade 6	
WRITTEN COMMUNICATION • Word derivations • Story sequence • Writing an outline • Writing a report	**STORY MESSAGES** • Main idea • Plot • Character • Setting • Dialogue • Diphthong • Digraph	**READING FOR A PURPOSE** • Critical thinking • Research data • Parables • Synonyms	LIFEPAC 1
SOUNDS TO WORDS • Hard and soft – c and g • Parts of dictionary • Accented syllables • Haiku Poetry	**MAIN IDEAS** • Poetry • Story • Synonyms • Compounds • Topic sentence • Adjectives • Nouns	**FORMING NEW WORDS** • Prefixes • Suffixes • Synonyms • Antonyms • Adjectives • Adverbs • Critical thinking	LIFEPAC 2
WORDS • HOW TO USE THEM • Prefixes • Suffixes • Homonyms • Antonyms • Poetry • Stories • Writing an outline	**WORDS TO STORIES** • Subject • Predicate • Adverbs • Idioms • Critical thinking • Writing a short story	**BETTER READING** • Story elements • Author's purpose • Information sources • Outline	LIFEPAC 3
MORE WORDS • HOW TO USE THEM • Parts of speech • Possession • Written directions • Verb tenses	**WRITTEN REPORT** • Outline • Four types of sentences • Metaphor • Simile • Writing the report	**SENTENCES** • Capitals • Punctuation • Four types of sentences • Author's purpose • Propaganda	LIFEPAC 4
WRITING FOR CLARITY • Figures of speech • Capital letters • Punctuation marks • Writing stories	**STORY ELEMENTS** • Legend • Implied meaning • Dialogue • Quotations • Word order • Usage • Critical thinking	**READING SKILLS** • Following directions • Literary forms • Phrases • Nouns • Verbs • Paragraph structure	LIFEPAC 5
FUN WITH FICTION • Book reports • Fiction • Nonfiction • Parables • Fables • Poetry	**POETRY** • Rhythm • Stanza • Symbolism • Personification • Irregular plurals	**POETRY** • Similes • Metaphors • Alliteration • Homonyms • Palindromes • Acronyms • Figures of speech	LIFEPAC 6
FACT AND FICTION • Nouns • Verbs • Contractions • Biography • Fables • Tall Tales	**WORD USAGE** • Nouns - common, plural, possessive • Fact • Opinion • Story • Main idea	**STORIES** • Story elements • Nouns • Pronouns • Vowel digraphs • Business letter	LIFEPAC 7
GRAMMAR AND WRITING • Adjectives to compare • Adverbs • Figurative language • Paragraphs	**ALL ABOUT VERBS** • Tense • Action • Participles • Of being • Regular • Irregular • Singular • Plural	**NEWSPAPERS** • Propaganda • News stories • Verbs – auxiliary, tenses • Adverbs	LIFEPAC 8
THE WRITTEN REPORT • Planning a report • Finding information • Outline • Writing a report	**READING FLUENCY** • Speed reading • Graphic aids • Study skills • Literary forms	**READING THE BIBLE** • Parables • Proverbs • Hebrew - poetry, prophecy • Bible history • Old Testament law	LIFEPAC 9
LOOKING BACK • Reading skills • Nouns • Adverbs • Written communication • Literary forms	**LOOKING BACK** • Literary forms • Parts of speech • Writing skills • Study skills	**LOOKING BACK** • Literary forms • Writing letters • Parts of speech • Punctuation	LIFEPAC 10

	Grade 7	Grade 8	Grade 9
LIFEPAC 1	**WORD USAGE** • Nouns – proper, common • Pronouns • Prefixes • Suffixes • Synonyms • Antonyms	**IMPROVE COMMUNICATION** • Roots • Inflections • Affixes • Interjections • Directions – oral, written • Non-verbal communication	**STRUCTURE OF LANGUAGE** • Nouns • Adjectives • Verbs • Prepositions • Adverbs • Conjunctions • Sentence parts
LIFEPAC 2	**MORE WORD USAGE** • Speech – stress, pitch • Verbs – tenses • Principle parts • Story telling	**ALL ABOUT ENGLISH** • Origin of language • Classification– nouns, pronouns, verbs, adjectives, adverbs	**NATURE OF LANGUAGE** • Origin of language • Use – oral and written • Dictionary • Writing a paper
LIFEPAC 3	**BIOGRAPHIES** • Biography as a form • Flashback technique • Deductive reasoning • Words – base, root	**PUNCTUATION AND WRITING** • Connecting and interrupting • The Essay • Thesis Statement	**PRACTICAL ENGLISH** • Dictionary use • Mnemonics • Writing a paper • Five minute speech
LIFEPAC 4	**LANGUAGE STRUCTURE** • Verbs – tenses • Principle parts • Sentence creativity • Speech – pitch, accent	**WORDS • HOW TO USE THEM** • Dictionary • Thesaurus • Accent • Diacritical mark • Standard • Nonstandard	**SHORT STORY FUNDAMENTALS** • Plot • Setting • Characterization • Conflict • Symbolism
LIFEPAC 5	**NATURE OF ENGLISH** • Formal • Informal • Redundant expressions • Verb tenses • Subject–verb agreement	**CORRECT LANGUAGE** • Using good form • Synonyms • Antonyms • Homonyms • Good speaking qualities	**LANGUAGE IN LITERATURE** • Collective Nouns • Verbs • Use of comparisons • Gerunds • Participles • Literary genres
LIFEPAC 6	**MECHANICS OF ENGLISH** • Punctuation • Complements • Modifiers • Clauses – subordinate, coordinate	**LANGUAGE AND LITERATURE** • History of English • Coordination and subordination • Autobiography	**MEANING IN PROSE AND POETRY** • Author's purpose and meaning • Meaning of structure • Factors of persuasion • Understanding poetry
LIFEPAC 7	**THE NOVEL** • The Hiding Place • Sequence of events • Author's purpose • Character sketch	**CRITICAL THINKING** • Word evaluation • The Paragraph – structure, coherence, introductory, concluding	**COMMUNICATION** • Planning a speech • Listening comprehension • Letters – business, informal, social
LIFEPAC 8	**LITERATURE** • Nonfiction • Listening skills • Commas • Semicolons • Nonverbal communications	**WRITE • LISTEN • READ** • Business letters • Personal letters • Four steps to listen • Nonfiction	**LIBRARY AND DRAMA** • Library resources • Drama – history, elements, reading • The Miracle Worker
LIFEPAC 9	**COMPOSITIONS** • Sentence types • Quality of paragraph • Pronunciation • Nonsense literature	**SPEAK AND WRITE** • Etymology • Modifiers • Person • Number • Tense • Oral report	**STUDIES IN THE NOVEL** • History • Define • Write • Critical essay • Twenty Thousand Leagues Under the Sea
LIFEPAC 10	**LOOKING BACK** • Parts of speech • Sentence structure • Punctuation • How to communicate	**LOOKING BACK** • Composition structure • Parts of speech • Critical thinking • Literary forms	**LOOKING BACK** • Communication – writing speaking, listening • Using resources • Literature review

Grade 10	Grade 11	Grade 12	
EVOLUTION OF ENGLISH • Historical development • Varieties of English • Substandard & standard • Changes in English	ENGLISH USES • VARIETIES • Standard • Nonstandard • Professional • Literary • Lexicography – purpose, bibliography	THE WORTH OF WORDS • Word categories • Expository writing • Sentence structure • Diction	LIFEPAC 1
LISTENING AND SPEAKING • Noun plurals • Suffixes • Creating a speech • Nature of listening	EFFECTIVE SENTENCES • Subordinate – clauses, conjunctions • Relative pronouns • Verbals • Appositives	STRUCTURE OF LANGUAGE • Parts of speech • Sentence structure • Subordinate phrases • Subordinate clauses	LIFEPAC 2
EFFECTIVE SENTENCES • Participles • Infinitives • Prepositions • Gerunds • Sentences – simple, compound, complex	SENTENCE WORKSHOP • Pronouns – personal, reference, agreement • Misplaced modifiers • Parallel structure	READ, RESEARCH, LISTEN • Reading skills • Resources for research • Taking notes • Drawing conclusions	LIFEPAC 3
POWER OF WORDS • Etymology • Connotations • Poetic devices • Poetry – literal, figurative, symbolic	WHY STUDY READING? • Greek and Latin roots • Diacritical markings • Finding the main idea • Analyzing a textbook	GIFT OF LANGUAGE • Origin–Biblical, • Koine Greek • Purpose of Grammar • Semantics	LIFEPAC 4
ELEMENTS OF COMPOSITION • Paragraphs • Connectives • Transitions • Expository writing – elements, ideas	POETRY • Metrical feet • Sets • Musical effects • Universality • Imagery • Connotation	ENGLISH LITERATURE • Early England • Medieval England • Fourteenth century • Chaucer	LIFEPAC 5
STRUCTURE AND READING • Subordinate clauses • Pronouns – gender, case, agreement • Reading for recognition	NONFICTION • Elements • Types – essays, diaries, newspaper, biography • Composition	ELIZABETHAN LITERATURE • Poetry • Prose • Drama • Essay	LIFEPAC 6
ORAL READING AND DRAMA • Skills of oral reading • Drama – history, irony elements, allegory • Everyman	AMERICAN DRAMA • Development • History • Structure • Purpose • Our Town	17TH—18TH CENTURY LITERATURE • Historical background • Puritan literature • Common sense – satire • Sensibility	LIFEPAC 7
THE SHORT STORY • Elements • Enjoying • Writing • The Literary Critique	AMERICAN NOVEL • Eighteenth, nineteenth twentieth century • The Old Man and the Sea • The Critical Essay	WRITING • SHORT STORY, POETRY • Fundamentals • Inspiration • Technique and style • Form and process	LIFEPAC 8
THE NOVEL • Elements • In His Steps • The Critical Essay • The Book Review	COMPOSITION • Stating the thesis • Research • Outline • Writing the paper	POETRY • ROMANTIC , VICTORIAN • Wordsworth • Coleridge • Gordon • Byron • Shelley • Keats • Tennyson • Hopkins • Robert and Elizabeth B Browning	LIFEPAC 9
LOOKING BACK • Writing skills • Speech skills • Poetry • Drama • Short stories • Novel	LOOKING BACK • Analyzing written word • Effective sentences • Expository prose • Genres of American literature	LOOKING BACK • Creative writing • English literature – Medieval to Victorian	LIFEPAC 10

MANAGEMENT

STRUCTURE OF THE LIFEPAC CURRICULUM

The LIFEPAC curriculum is conveniently structured to provide one teacher handbook containing teacher support material with answer keys and ten student worktexts for each subject at grade levels two through twelve. The worktext format of the LIFEPACs allows the student to read the textual information and complete workbook activities all in the same booklet. The easy to follow LIFEPAC numbering system lists the grade as the first number(s) and the last two digits as the number of the series. For example, the Language Arts LIFEPAC at the 6th grade level, 5th book in the series would be LA 605.

Each LIFEPAC is divided into 3 to 5 sections and begins with an introduction or overview of the booklet as well as a series of specific learning objectives to give a purpose to the study of the LIFEPAC. The introduction and objectives are followed by a vocabulary section which may be found at the beginning of each section at the lower levels, at the beginning of the LIFEPAC in the middle grades, or in the glossary at the high school level. Vocabulary words are used to develop word recognition and should not be confused with the spelling words introduced later in the LIFEPAC. The student should learn all vocabulary words before working the LIFEPAC sections to improve comprehension, retention, and reading skills.

Each activity or written assignment has a number for easy identification, such as 1.1. The first number corresponds to the LIFEPAC section and the number to the right of the decimal is the number of the activity.

Teacher checkpoints, which are essential to maintain quality learning, are found at various locations throughout the LIFEPAC. The teacher should check 1) neatness of work and penmanship, 2) quality of understanding (tested with a short oral quiz), 3) thoroughness of answers (complete sentences and paragraphs, correct spelling, etc.), 4) completion of activities (no blank spaces), and 5) accuracy of answers as compared to the answer key (all answers correct).

The self test questions are also number coded for easy reference. For example, 2.015 means that this is the 15th question in the self test of Section II. The first number corresponds to the LIFEPAC section, the zero indicates that it is a self test question, and the number to the right of the zero the question number.

The LIFEPAC test is packaged at the centerfold of each LIFEPAC. It should be removed and put aside before giving the booklet to the student for study.

Answer and test keys have the same numbering system as the LIFEPACs and appear at the back of this handbook. The student may be given access to the answer keys (not the test keys) under teacher supervision so that he can score his own work.

A thorough study of the Curriculum Overview by the teacher before instruction begins is essential to the success of the student. The teacher should become familiar with expected skill mastery and understand how these grade level skills fit into the overall skill development of the curriculum. The teacher should also preview the objectives that appear at the beginning of each LIFEPAC for additional preparation and planning.

TEST SCORING and GRADING

Answer keys and test keys give examples of correct answers. They convey the idea, but the student may use many ways to express a correct answer. The teacher should check for the essence of the answer, not for the exact wording. Many questions are high level and require thinking and creativity on the part of the student. Each answer should be scored based on whether or not the main idea written by the student matches the model example. "Any Order" or "Either Order" in a key indicates that no particular order is necessary to be correct.

Most self tests and LIFEPAC tests at the lower elementary levels are scored at 1 point per answer; however, the upper levels may have a point system awarding 2 to 5 points for various answers or questions. Further, the total test points will vary; they may not always equal 100 points. They may be 78, 85, 100, 105, etc.

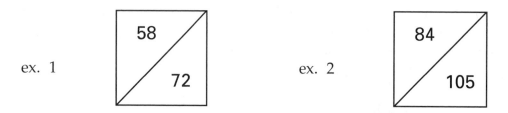

ex. 1   58 / 72   ex. 2   84 / 105

A score box similar to ex. 1 above is located at the end of each self test and on the front of the LIFEPAC test. The bottom score, 72, represents the total number of points possible on the test. The upper score, 58, represents the number of points your student will need to receive an 80% or passing grade. If you wish to establish the exact percentage that your student has achieved, find the total points of his correct answers and divide it by the bottom number (in this case 72.) For example, if your student has a point total of 65, divide 65 by 72 for a grade of 90%. Referring to ex. 2, on a test with a total of 105 possible points, the student would have to receive a minimum of 84 correct points for an 80% or passing grade. If your student has received 93 points, simply divide the 93 by 105 for a percentage grade of 89%. Students who receive a score below 80% should review the LIFEPAC and retest using the appropriate Alternate Test found in the Teacher's Guide.

The following is a guideline to assign letter grades for completed LIFEPACs based on a maximum total score of 100 points.

LIFEPAC Test   =   60% of the Total Score (or percent grade)
Self Test   =   25% of the Total Score (average percent of self tests)
Reports   =   10% or 10* points per LIFEPAC
Oral Work   =   5% or 5* points per LIFEPAC
*Determined by the teacher's subjective evaluation of the student's daily work.

Example:

LIFEPAC Test Score	=	92%	92	x	.60	=	55 points
Self Test Average	=	90%	90	x	.25	=	23 points
Reports						=	8 points
Oral Work						=	4 points

TOTAL POINTS = 90 points

Grade Scale based on point system:

100	–	94	=	A
93	–	86	=	B
85	–	77	=	C
76	–	70	=	D
Below		70	=	F

TEACHER HINTS and STUDYING TECHNIQUES

LIFEPAC Activities are written to check the level of understanding of the preceding text. The student may look back to the text as necessary to complete these activities; however, a student should never attempt to do the activities without reading (studying) the text first. Self tests and LIFEPAC tests are never open book tests.

Language arts activities (skill integration) often appear within other subject curriculum. The purpose is to give the student an opportunity to test his skill mastery outside of the context in which it was presented.

Writing complete answers (paragraphs) to some questions is an integral part of the LIFEPAC Curriculum in all subjects. This builds communication and organization skills, increases understanding and retention of ideas, and helps enforce good penmanship. Complete sentences should be encouraged for this type of activity. Obviously, single words or phrases do not meet the intent of the activity, since multiple lines are given for the response.

Review is essential to student success. Time invested in review where review is suggested will be time saved in correcting errors later. Self tests, unlike the section activities, are closed book. This procedure helps to identify weaknesses before they become too great to overcome. Certain objectives from self tests are cumulative and test previous sections; therefore, good preparation for a self test must include all material studied up to that testing point.

The following procedure checklist has been found to be successful in developing good study habits in the LIFEPAC curriculum.

1. Read the introduction and Table of Contents.
2. Read the objectives.
3. Recite and study the entire vocabulary (glossary) list.
4. Study each section as follows:
    a. Read the introduction and study the section objectives.
    b. Read all the text for the entire section, but answer none of the activities.
    c. Return to the beginning of the section and memorize each vocabulary word and definition.
    d. Reread the section, complete the activities, check the answers with the answer key, correct all errors, and have the teacher check.
    e. Read the self test but do not answer the questions.
    f. Go to the beginning of the first section and reread the text and answers to the activities up to the self test you have not yet done.
    g. Answer the questions to the self test without looking back.
    h. Have the self test checked by the teacher.
    i. Correct the self test and have the teacher check the corrections.
    j. Repeat steps a–i for each section.

5. Use the SQ3R* method to prepare for the LIFEPAC test.
6. Take the LIFEPAC test as a closed book test.
7. LIFEPAC tests are administered and scored under direct teacher supervision. Students who receive scores below 80% should review the LIFEPAC using the SQ3R* study method and take the Alternate Test located in the Teacher Handbook. The final test grade may be the grade on the Alternate Test or an average of the grades from the original LIFEPAC test and the Alternate Test.

> *SQ3R: **S**can the whole LIFEPAC.
> **Q**uestion yourself on the objectives.
> **R**ead the whole LIFEPAC again.
> **R**ecite through an oral examination.
> **R**eview weak areas.

GOAL SETTING and SCHEDULES

Each school must develop its own schedule, because no single set of procedures will fit every situation. The following is an example of a daily schedule that includes the five LIFEPAC subjects as well as time slotted for special activities.

Possible Daily Schedule

8:15	–	8:25	Pledges, prayer, songs, devotions, etc.
8:25	–	9:10	Bible
9:10	–	9:55	Language Arts
9:55	–	10:15	Recess (juice break)
10:15	–	11:00	Mathematics
11:00	–	11:45	Social Studies
11:45	–	12:30	Lunch, recess, quiet time
12:30	–	1:15	Science
1:15	–		Drill, remedial work, enrichment*

*Enrichment: Computer time, physical education, field trips, fun reading, games and puzzles, family business, hobbies, resource persons, guests, crafts, creative work, electives, music appreciation, projects.

Basically, two factors need to be considered when assigning work to a student in the LIFEPAC curriculum.

The first is time. An average of 45 minutes should be devoted to each subject, each day. Remember, this is only an average. Because of extenuating circumstances a student may spend only 15 minutes on a subject one day and the next day spend 90 minutes on the same subject.

The second factor is the number of pages to be worked in each subject. A single LIFEPAC is designed to take 3 to 4 weeks to complete. Allowing about 3-4 days for LIFEPAC introduction, review, and tests, the student has approximately 15 days to complete the LIFEPAC pages. Simply take the number of pages in the LIFEPAC, divide it by 15 and you will have the number of pages that must be completed on a daily basis to keep the student on schedule. For example, a LIFEPAC containing 45 pages will require 3 completed pages per day. Again, this is only an average. While working a 45 page LIFEPAC, the student may complete only 1 page the first day if the text has a lot of activities or reports, but go on to complete 5 pages the next day.

Long range planning requires some organization. Because the traditional school year originates in the early fall of one year and continues to late spring of the following year, a calendar should be devised that covers this period of time. Approximate beginning and completion dates can be noted on the calendar as well as special occasions such as holidays, vacations and birthdays. Since each LIFEPAC takes 3-4 weeks or eighteen days to complete, it should take about 180 school days to finish a set of ten LIFEPACs. Starting at the beginning school date, mark off eighteen school days on the calendar and that will become the targeted completion date for the first LIFEPAC. Continue marking the calendar until you have established dates for the remaining nine LIFEPACs making adjustments for previously noted holidays and vacations. If all five subjects are being used, the ten established target dates should be the same for the LIFEPACs in each subject.

FORMS

The sample weekly lesson plan and student grading sheet forms are included in this section as teacher support materials and may be duplicated at the convenience of the teacher.

The student grading sheet is provided for those who desire to follow the suggested guidelines for assignment of letter grades found on page 3 of this section. The student's self test scores should be posted as percentage grades. When the LIFEPAC is completed the teacher should average the self test grades, multiply the average by .25 and post the points in the box marked self test points. The LIFEPAC percentage grade should be multiplied by .60 and posted. Next, the teacher should award and post points for written reports and oral work. A report may be any type of written work assigned to the student whether it is a LIFEPAC or additional learning activity. Oral work includes the student's ability to respond orally to questions which may or may not be related to LIFEPAC activities or any type of oral report assigned by the teacher. The points may then be totaled and a final grade entered along with the date that the LIFEPAC was completed.

The Student Record Book which was specifically designed for use with the Alpha Omega curriculum provides space to record weekly progress for one student over a nine week period as well as a place to post self test and LIFEPAC scores. The Student Record Books are available through the current Alpha Omega catalog; however, unlike the enclosed forms these books are not for duplication and should be purchased in sets of four to cover a full academic year.

WEEKLY LESSON PLANNER

Week of:

Subject	Subject	Subject	Subject
Monday			

Subject	Subject	Subject	Subject
Tuesday			

Subject	Subject	Subject	Subject
Wednesday			

Subject	Subject	Subject	Subject
Thursday			

Subject	Subject	Subject	Subject
Friday			

WEEKLY LESSON PLANNER

Week of:

	Subject	Subject	Subject	Subject
Monday				
	Subject	Subject	Subject	Subject
Tuesday				
	Subject	Subject	Subject	Subject
Wednesday				
	Subject	Subject	Subject	Subject
Thursday				
	Subject	Subject	Subject	Subject
Friday				

Student Name _____   Year _____

Bible

LP #	Self Test Scores by Sections 1	2	3	4	5	Self Test Points	LIFEPAC Test	Oral Points	Report Points	Final Grade	Date
01											
02											
03											
04											
05											
06											
07											
08											
09											
10											

History & Geography

LP #	Self Test Scores by Sections 1	2	3	4	5	Self Test Points	LIFEPAC Test	Oral Points	Report Points	Final Grade	Date
01											
02											
03											
04											
05											
06											
07											
08											
09											
10											

Language Arts

LP #	Self Test Scores by Sections 1	2	3	4	5	Self Test Points	LIFEPAC Test	Oral Points	Report Points	Final Grade	Date
01											
02											
03											
04											
05											
06											
07											
08											
09											
10											

Student Name _____   Year _____

Mathematics

LP #	Self Test Scores by Sections 1	2	3	4	5	Self Test Points	LIFEPAC Test	Oral Points	Report Points	Final Grade	Date
01											
02											
03											
04											
05											
06											
07											
08											
09											
10											

Science

LP #	Self Test Scores by Sections 1	2	3	4	5	Self Test Points	LIFEPAC Test	Oral Points	Report Points	Final Grade	Date
01											
02											
03											
04											
05											
06											
07											
08											
09											
10											

Spelling/Electives

LP #	Self Test Scores by Sections 1	2	3	4	5	Self Test Points	LIFEPAC Test	Oral Points	Report Points	Final Grade	Date
01											
02											
03											
04											
05											
06											
07											
08											
09											
10											

NOTES

INSTRUCTIONS FOR LANGUAGE ARTS

The LIFEPAC curriculum from grades two through twelve is structured so that the daily instructional material is written directly into the LIFEPACs. The student is encouraged to read and follow this instructional material in order to develop independent study habits. The teacher should introduce the LIFEPAC to the student, set a required completion schedule, complete teacher checks, be available for questions regarding both content and procedures, administer and grade tests, and develop additional learning activities as desired. Teachers working with several students may schedule their time so that students are assigned to a quiet work activity when it is necessary to spend instructional time with one particular student.

Language arts includes those subjects that develop the students' communication skills. The LIFEPAC approach to combining reading, spelling, penmanship, composition, grammar, speech and literature in a single unit allows the teacher to integrate the study of these various language arts subject areas. The variety and scope of the curriculum may make it difficult for students to complete the required material within the suggested daily scheduled time of forty-five minutes. Spelling, book reports and various forms of composition may need to be completed during the afternoon enrichment period.

This section of the language arts Teacher's Guide includes the following teacher aids: *Book Report Form*, *Books Read Chart*, Suggested and Required Material (supplies), and Additional Learning Activities.

The *Book Report Form* and the *Books Read Chart* may be duplicated for individual student use.

The materials section refers only to LIFEPAC materials and does not include materials which may be needed for the additional learning activities. Additional learning activities provide a change from the daily school routine, encourage the student's interest in learning and may be used as a reward for good study habits.

BOOK REPORT FORM

Title _____   Your Name _____

Author _____   Date _____

Illustrator _____   Principal Characters _____

Number of Pages _____   _____

Copyright Date _____   _____

Fiction or Nonfiction _____   Setting _____

Summary: A summary gives the important events of a story or book. It skips most of the details but a few make the report more interesting. The summary should be written in complete sentences.

_____

_____

_____

_____

_____

_____

_____

_____

_____

_____

_____

_____

Tell why you did or did not like the book.

_____

_____

_____

_____

_____

_____

_____

_____

Name: _____

BOOKS READ

Title: Author: Date:	Title: Author: Date:	Title: Author: Date:	Title: Author: Date:
Title: Author: Date:	Title: Author: Date:	Title: Author: Date:	Title: Author: Date:
Title: Author: Date:	Title: Author: Date:	Title: Author: Date:	Title: Author: Date:
Title: Author: Date:	Title: Author: Date:	Title: Author: Date:	Title: Author: Date:
Title: Author: Date:	Title: Author: Date:	Title: Author: Date:	Title: Author: Date:
Title: Author: Date:	Title: Author: Date:	Title: Author: Date:	Title: Author: Date:
Title: Author: Date:	Title: Author: Date:	Title: Author: Date:	Title: Author: Date:
Title: Author: Date:	Title: Author: Date:	Title: Author: Date:	Title: Author: Date:
Title: Author: Date:	Title: Author: Date:	Title: Author: Date:	Title: Author: Date:

Materials Needed for LIFEPAC

Required:

Suggested:
The Holy Bible, King James Version
World Book Dictionary
concordance
Roget's Thesaurus
Leslie, Louis A. T*wenty Thousand Words*
 Spelled and Divided for Quick Reference. New
 York: McGraw-Hill Book Company, 1971. Or
 latest Edition
Strunk, William and White, E.B. *Elements of*
 Style. Mac Millian Publishing Co., Inc., 1979.
 Third or latest Edition
Handbook of Style. University of Chicago
 Press, 1993. Or latest Edition

Extended Writing Assignment

Be certain that each student completes every step required by this assignment and prepares his paper in the form described in the *Form and Mechanics* section of this LIFEPAC. You may wish to check informally at the outline stage (Adult check). Remind students that the third step, revision, may be the most important step. If students conscientiously mark off each item of the Revision Chart, found near the end of Section III, they will be able to correct errors and to improve their papers. You may wish to duplicate this Revision Chart for use with all longer papers in the English 1200 series.

Some general notes about grading papers may be helpful. Reading the entire paper before marking errors will give the teacher an overall grasp of the student's purpose or direction. Many teachers skim the entire class's papers to assess the response to an assignment and to gauge superior and inferior work before assigning an individual grade. Many teachers prefer using a lead pencil instead of red ink or red pencil. Too many corrections tend to discourage or confuse students; it may be helpful to concentrate on one major area of problems (sentence structure, pronouns, or whatever is introduced in the appropriate LIFEPAC) keeping in mind that the writing communicating effort is a cumulative skill and should be graded as such.

After reading a paper, review the assignment in your mind. Many teachers feel that the completion of an assignment is an average grade; if the student has not addressed the assignment, then he is graded poorly or is asked to repeat the assignment. Logic in presenting the assignment, clarity of thought, and precision of word choice are three major considerations to be weighed before assigning a grade. Correct and clear sentence structure, grammatical correctness, appropriate punctuation, and correct spelling should also be considered, with strengths in these areas influencing a higher grade and deficiencies calling for a lower grade. An average paper should meet all the prescribed standards. Superior papers should demonstrate superior effort, both in mechanics and form and in content and creativity.

The first paper should help locate student weaknesses in expression and organization, as well as in grammar and mechanics. This assignment can provide some helpful ideas about future papers, clarifying what the student should be working toward. Each paper should have a title and several paragraphs that adequately develop the student's ideas. The first paragraph should contain introductory material and the central idea (thesis) to be developed. Each paragraph then should logically develop an aspect of that central idea, an aspect that is usually stated as a topic sentence. The paper should have a definite conclusion; it should not just stop. After reading the paper through, once for content and once for errors, you will be ready to assign a grade. Many teachers give a "content" grade and a "mechanics" grade; others, however, feel that those two aspects should be integrated into a well written paper. Clarify your own stand, make it known to your students, then be consistent and fair in your grading. Communication is one of the most important skills available to mankind; it is certainly a challenge to teach students to write well. Additionally, it is a real pleasure to help students learn to explore their own ideas and then to communicate those ideas to other people.

Additional Learning Activities
Section I Word Study
1. Instill excitement about making words by approaching word wheels (pages 3 through 8) as a game. Have the students draw wheels on the chalkboard. The student should work the wheels at his desk before he tackles one on the board. Make the activity a simple brainstorming procedure, with each one thinking up as many words out of his own vocabulary as possible. Do not let anyone use the answer key until all other sources have been exhausted. Keep the answer keys at your desk until this part of the LIFEPAC is nearly completed.
2. The most efficient way for students to form new words is to go down the list of prefixes in the LIFEPAC and to try them in front of their roots. This is not an exhaustive list, but students will find a pattern of the prefixes most commonly used: *ab-, ad-, come, con-, de-, e-, exe, in-*(not), *in-*(into, within), *inter-, per-, pre-, re-, retro-, sub* and *trans-*. Then a shifting of suffixes creates new words. If students are not sure that a combination they form is a bonafide word, have them look it up in the dictionary. Suggest that they involve their families. Students may be surprised at how many words their parents know that they do not. When students discover they can form actual words from roots and prefixes, they may want to start a vocabulary notebook. Have them allow a couple of pages for each letter of the alphabet, write the new word, and provide a short definition.
3. Games such as *Scrabble* and *Probe* will provide places to use some of this information. These games should improve spelling. Spelling of words like *interrogate* becomes more understandable when the student puts *inter* with *rog* and sees the two r's together. He knows why there should be two r's, not one.
4. Test the mastery of the roots and affixes. Duplicate a master list of roots. Have students who wish to excel and who wish to test themselves supply the meaning of each root or affix and at least two English words that employ that root or affix. Rote learning appeals to certain kinds of students; it is much more difficult for others. It provides an excellent opportunity for mental discipline along with the other positive enrichment advantages.

Section II Expository Writing
1. Use a *Nelson-Denny Reading Test* to obtain percentiles on the vocabulary capability of every student. Your school may have other means for testing vocabulary; if so, use them, unless the students have already taken these diagnostic tests. Such tests need to be ones whose percentiles are calibrated on national norms for the sake of reliability. Give the students their scores on such tests.
2. A grading session often helps students improve their writing since they learn another point of view and more objectivity. Sometimes they also become aware of the difficulties involved in grading papers. Have students duplicate their essays; you receive the original, and they may work with the copies. Have students work in small groups. Each student should carefully read the paper of another student, then go over the paper using the guides found in the *Form and Mechanics* section and near the end of Section III in LIFEPAC. You may also decide to read the class the teacher's material accompanying the Extended Writing Assignment to give students some basic grading guidelines. You may wish to incorporate the students' grades with your own.

3. Choose a general topic, such as Christianity, love, faith, and so forth. Break your topic down into more limited topics.

4. British preacher Sydney Smith once said, "The writer does the most who gives his reader the most knowledge and takes from him the least time." If this quotation could be engraved on the minds of young writers and could be applied to every particle of their writing, then tremendous strides would be accomplished toward good writing. If you have an artist in the class, perhaps he or she could letter the quote on a strip of posterboard, and mount it in the classroom.

Section III Sentence Structure, Diction, and Usage

1. Integrate the sections of this LIFEPAC. The information about technical and scientific words, literary and music terms, and for some students, the mathematical terminology, can act as springboards for writing. Students, through their parents, may have access to knowledge of many other fields of work that have their own jargon. Each student should research a different line of work, and write about it. A "Chronicle of Careers" could be collated for everyone to read and enjoy. This effort could initiate a continuing project with class after class adding to it. Made available to the whole school, this "Chronicle" could inform lower classmen of opportunities in the job fields that appeal to them in a way unique from all other job compilations.

2. Arrange a project similar to the group activity for Section II. Place the students in small groups, give them copies of previously written, ungraded paragraphs, to exchange, and read. Have them look for problems with parallel structure, fragments, and run-on sentences, and with any of the other errors described in Section III.

3. If you normally do not allow students to rewrite their papers for a higher grade, you may consider suggesting rewrites for this portion of the class since the LIFEPAC is concerned with revision and correction of errors.

Materials Needed for LIFEPAC:

Required:

Suggested:
The Holy Bible, King James Version
literature anthology, any approved edition
current newspaper or magazine
Strunk, William and White, E.B. *Elements of Style.* Mac Millian Publishing Co., Inc., 1979. Third or latest Edition
Handbook of Style. University of Chicago Press, 1993. Or latest Edition

The teacher should carefully screen any suggested anthologies for unacceptable selections before making them available to the students. Teacher should also be familiar with any suggested student literature to assure that each selection is suitable.

Extended Writing Assignment In The LIFEPAC

This paper should reflect a variety of sentence patterns and the use of proper subordination. See extended Writing Assignment, section 1201 of this handbook for grading guidelines.

Additional Learning Activities
  Section I Parts of Speech
1. Write five sentences on the board. Ask the students to identify the eight parts of speech in each sentence.
2. Write a number of short sentences on the board, for example, "The man walked across the street." Ask the students to add adjectives and adverbs to make the sentence more interesting, for example, "The crippled old man walked hesitatingly across the busy city street."
3. Have students write the eight parts of speech on pieces of paper. Fold them and put them in a box and have the students select one. They then play, "Who am I?" giving clues to its identity by using that part of speech in a sentence or giving the definition of that part of speech.
4. Have the students write five sentences with blanks in place of all the nouns and adjectives. (Have all the students leave the same amount of blanks and number each one—l, 2, 3, etc.) Ask the students to list and number possible nouns and adjectives on a separate piece of paper. Students should then exchange the sentences with each other and fill in the numbered blanks with their matching numbered nouns and adjectives. This exercise should result in some humorous sentences. Share the sentences with the class.
5. Write five of your favorite Bible verses. Write the abbreviation for the part of speech above each word.
6. Copy five sentences from a literature text. Then rewrite the sentences using proper nouns in place of all the pronouns. Notice how awkward this makes the sentences.
  Section II The Structure of Sentences
1. Write the following five sentences on the board. Have the students delete the modification so that only the skeletal, S + V pattern sentences remain.
    a. Some of the sheep were lost in the pasture.
    b. We're hoping for much milder weather soon.
    c. A man with high ideals works for the good of mankind.
    d. He ran into his room and lay down.
    e. Some hungry children were standing on the steps.

2. Write the following five sentences on the board. Have the students expand each sentence by modification and compounding.
   a. The boy won.
   b. The soldiers marched.
   c. Poverty still exists in the city.
   d. The hotel is burning.
   e. Winter has arrived.
3. Cut an action picture out of a newspaper or magazine. Decide what is happening in the picture and what kind of people are involved. Write three S + V pattern sentences and three S + V + DO pattern sentences about the picture. Be descriptive and vary your sentence structure. Circle the words or groups of words that make up the skeletal sentence.
4. Look through a recent newspaper and find five examples of S + V + DO sentences. Discuss them with the rest of the class. If possible, find a cartoon with a caption. Clip and post on the bulletin board.
5. Copy five sentences out of your literature text. Take out all modifications and reduce each sentence to a skeletal sentence with subject and verb only.
6. Write an account in 150 to 200 words of your experiences in the private world of feelings, imaginations, or dreams. Use a good selection of adjectives to make it more interesting. Some ideas you might use are listed below.
   a. Would you make a good or a bad member of a flight crew? What if you were hijacked?
   b. What do you think of hunting? Is it wrong for people to kill animals?
   c. What are some of the things that suddenly pop into your mind when you cannot sleep?
   d. Are you sometimes fed up with the planet Earth? What kind of planet would you want instead?

Section III Methods of Subordination

1. Have students copy and complete each of these sentences, using a gerund or gerund phrase.
   a. He reached California by _____.
   b. _____ will never make you popular.
   c. Most people enjoy _____.
   d. _____ is the best way to lose weight
   e. I am concerned about his _____.
2. Have students copy and complete each of these sentences using infinitive phrases.
   a. It is natural for a boy his age _____.
   b. We wanted _____.
   c. I am not waiting any longer _____.
   d. The best place _____ is a quiet room.
   e. Does everyone in this class want _____ ?
3. Play a game to test your abilities. Select one classmate to be *It*. It stands in front of class, says a part of speech, points to someone, and counts to ten. The person to whom he points must give an example of that part of speech before It counts to ten. If he cannot, he takes the place of *It* and the game continues.

4. *Which one does not fit*? Using the eight parts of speech, each student writes four words for each of the eight with one word being incorrect (for example, noun—apple, book, dog, run). Can the other students spot the incorrect word? Pass the papers around the class and have other students select the incorrect words. Check the answers.

5. Look through a newspaper and find a short article that you can expand into a longer piece of writing. Think of which point of view you want to use, what tone you want to reflect, and rewrite the article in 250 words.

Materials Needed for LIFEPAC
Required: Suggested:

Extended Writing Assignment In The LIFEPAC

Grade this paper according to the detailed guidelines in the Extended Writing Assignment of the 1201 section of this handbook. Also check the research and note taking techniques to insure that the student has correctly mastered these pre-writing skills. A paper must first be well researched before it can be well written.

Additional Learning Activities
Section I Reading for Comprehension
1. Go over in class any of the drills in this section that the students originally found difficult. Concentrate on the areas that individual students have problems with and try to eliminate those problems.
2. Divide the class into groups and give each group examples of the six kinds of expository writing. Have each group identify which pattern their particular examples fit and state the reasons for that identification.
3. Have each student find (from another LIFEPAC or textbook) an example of one of those six patterns of exposition. Then have the student complete the following steps:
   a. identify the pattern,
   b. locate the topic sentence,
   c. rephrase the main idea in his own words, and
   d. point out the supporting details (or examples, illustrations, etc.) used to prove the thesis of the paragraph.

Section II Searching for Information
1. Organize a field trip to the nearest library for a student tour. Be certain to arrange this activity in advance with the librarian. She may prefer to conduct the tour herself. Include the card catalog or computerized card catalog, Readers' Guide, stacks, and newspaper and magazine sections in the tour.
2. Hold a class question-and-answer period about locating information in the library so that students can clear up any misunderstandings about research procedures.
3. Divide the class into groups. Assign each group a specific subject for research. By the following class period, each group should bring to class a list of at least five possible sources for researching its particular subject. The research information itself is not necessary; this is an exercise in locating sources to search any given topic.
4. Assign each student a specific topic (a book title, an author, a subject, etc.) and send him to the library card catalog. Have him locate and list at least six sources for his subject, including book or article title, author, publication data, and number of pages. These lists should be turned in.

Section III Listening for Information
1. Give a brief class lecture on any of the subjects covered in the literature LIFEPACs of this 1200 series. Have the students take notes during this lecture. Allow them to take these rough notes home overnight and revise them. Then grade the revised versions and return the graded copies with appropriate criticism to the students.
2. Invite an outside speaker to visit the class for a guest lecture (for example, a local minister, mayor, or civil organization officer). Have the students take notes on this lecture, revise them, and exchange them for grading. These graded copies should then be checked over by the teacher.
3. Have each student read an approved article outside of class and take notes on that article. These notes should be turned in and graded for completeness, clarity, and organization.

Materials Needed for LIFEPAC
    Required:

Suggested:
The Holy Bible, King James Version other versions of the Bible if available and permitted

Extended Writing Assignment In The LIFEPAC

This paper should be graded according to the detailed guidelines presented in Section V of English handbook 1201. In addition, this paper should be examined for content, to insure that the student has properly classified his usage of language and meaning, and for organization. Look for concise (the limit is two pages) organization of the material and the use of transitional words and phrases to link paragraphs.

Additional Learning Activities
Section I Origin of Language
1. Invite a local minister to address the class concerning the Biblical origins of language. Schedule a question-and-answer session after the talk and encourage class participation.
2. To illustrate changing language, obtain several versions of The Holy Bible (King James, New International Version, etc.) from the library. Divide the class into groups and assign each group the same Biblical chapter (for example, the story of Noah). Let each group choose a representative to read aloud its version of the story in class. Then hold a group discussion comparing the differences in language and phrasing.
3. Assign each student ten words to look up first in a modern dictionary and then in a much older one (if possible, the original Webster or a very early edition). Set aside a class period when the students can bring their lists to class and compare them.

Section II Grammar
1. Locate a copy of a very early grammar book used in England or America. Share portions of it with the class to illustrate how our language and its structure is constantly changing.
2. Organize a class debate or discussion on the subject "traditional grammar versus structural grammar." One-half of the group should advocate traditional views and the other half support the structural theories.
3. Have each student pick a page from any one of his other LIFEPACs or textbooks. The student should then identify every pronoun on the page and correctly classify it according to nominative, objective, or possessive case.

Section III Semantics
1. Find and bring to class one of the twelve volumes of the Oxford English Dictionary (or the single volume abridged copy if the first is unavailable) and pass it around among the students. Go over its usage in class.
2. Using the ten examples from Activity 3.32 of this LIFEPAC, have each student choose his best ad and bring it to class. Let the students exchange ads and lead a discussion of the different usages of the words involved. Point out how the context of usage so often determines the meaning in each individual case.
3. Give each student a list of five words (or have them choose five) to look up in the Oxford English Dictionary. Students should then write and turn in brief paragraphs summarizing the history of each word on their lists. If class time permits, some of the more interesting histories could be shared in class.

Materials Needed for Lifepac
Required:

Suggested:
dictionary
an encyclopedia series or an anthology of
 medieval literature
The Holy Bible, King James Version
copy of a translation of *Beowulf*
Scott, Sir Walter. *Ivanhoe*. New York: E. P.
 Dutton. A colorful story of knights,
 tournaments, chivalry, and castles of the
 Middle Ages.
Scott, Sir Walter. *The Talisman*. New York:
 E. P. Dutton. An adventure about knights
 and the crusades. Two strong adversaries
 learn about each other.
Stevenson, Robert Lewis. *The Black Arrow*.
 Bridgeport, CT: Airmont Publishing
 Company, Inc., 1964. An easy-to-read story
 of adventure set against the War of Roses.
Eliot, T.S. *Murder in the Cathedral*. New York:
 Harcourt, Brace, Jovanovich, Inc. 1964
 The account of Thomas á Becket's
 martyrdom in poetic form, a drama

Extended Writing Assignment

1. Activity 3.32 is the first lengthy paper in this LIFEPAC. Possible situations teachers could suggest for student use include these ideas:
   a. several patients waiting in a doctor's office,
   b. passengers on an airliner or train, or
   c. a varied group on an organized tourist tour.
   In short, any situation in which people of varied backgrounds would be "thrown together" would provide a suitable framework for the paper. This paper should, of course, be graded according to the mechanical criteria in Section 1201 of this handbook. Creativity is of prime importance; therefore, this particular paper should be graded chiefly on content. Make certain that the students follow Chaucer's form in their "Prologue" but allow wide latitude in developing the characters to encourage creativity.
2. Content is more important in this paper than creativity. The student must do research to be familiar with the history and background of the Middle Ages to relate those specifics to his reading selection. He should also document any Christian principles he discusses with Scriptural references whenever possible. Make certain that any points selected are documented from the text. Again, logical order and clear presentation are important.

Additional Learning Activities
  Section I Early England
     1. Bring an Old English copy of *Beowulf* to class and read aloud portions to the class. If time permits, pass the copy around and let several students try their hands at reading. This experience will illustrate the differences and similarities in Old English and modern speech.

2. Stage a scene from *Beowulf* in class. If time permits, act out several scenes, changing the cast so that more of the students can participate. Discuss the differences in this kind of a scene and drama today.

3. Have the students try their hands at writing one of the following types of literature:
   a. several riddles,
   b. a gnome, or
   c. a very brief elegy.

Section II Medieval England

1. Locate a film or book on the Norman Conquest of England and share it with the class. This information will complement the brief sketch of the Norman Invasion in this LIFEPAC and will give the students a more detailed background of this crucial period of English history. Such a background will help students to understand the literature of these times as well as the development of modern English.

2. Locate and bring to class a copy of the Magna Carta and one of the Declaration of Independence. Organize a class discussion covering the differences and similarities between the two documents.

3. Have each student choose one of the following topics to research. Students should present a brief oral or written report to the class about their findings.
   a. The New Middle Class
   b. The Growth of Towns
   c. The Role of the Church
   d. The Feudal Society
   e. The Life Style of the Nobility
   f. The French Influence After A.D. 1066
   g. The Crusades

Section III Fourteenth-Century England

1. Find a copy of either *Sir Gawain and the Green Knight* or *The Pearl* and read portions of it to the class. Encourage comparisons between this literature and Chaucer's *Canterbury Tales*.

2. In LIFEPAC Activity 3.32 the students wrote fictional "Prologues" of their own. Choose several of the best (possibly three or four) and stage the scene in the classroom. Again, encourage student participation and lead a discussion comparing these "Prologues" with Chaucer's.

3. Have each student pick five words from Chaucer's works (example, *bygynneth*) in Middle English and trace the changes in spellings and meanings of those words to the present-day usage.

Materials Needed for LIFEPAC

Required:
Shakespeare, William. *Hamlet*, edited
by David Bevington
New York: Bantam Books 1988
(or any other available edition of
the play).

Suggested:
dictionary
The Holy Bible, King James Version
Chute, Marchette. *An Introduction to
Shakespeare*. New York: E. P. Dutton and
Company, Inc., 1951. Or Similar Book.

The teacher should carefully screen any suggested anthologies or texts for unacceptable selections before making them available to students. Teachers should also be familiar with any suggested student literature to assure that each selection is suitable.

Extended Writing Assignment In The LIFEPAC

1. Grade this report according to the general grading guidelines in the Extended Writing Assignment, section 1201 of this handbook. Also check this paper for these specific points:
   a. to insure that the student has adequately researched his subject,
   b. to determine that he has included all the research information necessary in his report,
   c. to check the accuracy of that information,
   d. to grade the organization of the material, and
   e. to determine if the student's presentation is clear and concise.

2. Activity 3.21. This essay should be graded mechanically according to the detailed guidelines in this handbook, section 1201, as well as the criteria set forth in this LIFEPAC, Section III. See that the student has followed his own outline in the organization of his paper and that he has developed his thesis logically and clearly. Make certain that his points are supported by the play's text, and check to see that the paper's conclusion is a logical result of the paper and the thesis statement. Mechanics are important, but content is vital, and the organization of material is particularly meaningful in a critical paper. The logic of the student's presentation determines the effectiveness of his critical argument.

Additional Learning Activities
Section I Elizabethan Poetry and Prose
1. Locate and bring to class several more modern sonnets (W. H. Auden, for example, wrote several). Read them aloud and lead a class discussion comparing these selections with the Elizabethan sonnets in this LIFEPAC.
2. Organize a class discussion centered around the King James Version of the Bible and a modern translation. Divide the class into several groups and have each group pick out a certain chapter, parable, or psalm, and look it up in both versions. Compare the language, style, and word usage of the identical passages in the two different versions.
3. Have each student locate one of the following works and bring a copy to share with the class:
   a. an essay by Francis Bacon,
   b. a poem by John Donne not in this LIFEPAC,
   c. a sonnet by Shakespeare not in this LIFEPAC, or
   d. an Elizabethan song not in this LIFEPAC.

Section II Elizabethan Drama

1. If time permits, share with the class portions or all of play—mystery, morality, or miracle—from the Middle Ages. Point out similarities and differences between that play and *Hamlet*.

2. Have the class stage a scene (or several scenes) from a morality, mystery, or miracle play of the Middle Ages. (*Everyman* is a good choice because of the availability of the text.)

3. Have each student build, draw, or obtain sketches or photographs of one of the Elizabethan theaters. Set aside a class period so that the models and drawings can be shared by the entire class.

Section III The Critical Essay

1. Select one or two criticisms of Shakespeare's *Hamlet* and read them aloud in class. Encourage class discussion of the viewpoints of the essays. Do the students agree with this interpretation of the play? If not, why?

2. Have the students share in class the critical essays they wrote for Activity 3.21. (This can be done before or after the teacher has graded the paper.) Hold class discussions on the essays. Do the students seem to share the same opinions, or do they widely differ? Are they basing their points of view on evidence from the play? Encourage the students to constructively criticize each other's papers.

3. Let more ambitious students choose a critical essay to read outside of class and prepare an oral report summarizing the essay he read. (Possible choices are T. S. Eliot, Sir Francis Bacon, Samuel Johnson, Percy Bysshe Shelley, or Matthew Arnold.)

Materials Needed for LIFEPAC
    Required:

    Suggested:
    The Holy Bible, King James Version
    Bunyan, John. *Pilgrim's Progress*. Chicago:
     Moody Press.
    Milton, John. "Book XII," *Paradise Lost, a New*
     Edition: A Poem in Twelve Books. Merrit Y.
     Hughes, editor. Indianapolis, IN: Odyssey
     Press, 1962. Or Newer Edition
    Swift, Jonathan. *Gulliver's Travels*. New York.
     Penguin Books, Inc, 1967(or latest edition).

EXTENDED WRITING ASSIGNMENT

This essay, like all others in this LIFEPAC, should first be graded using the guidelines in section 1201 of this handbook. Additionally, this paper should be judged on the specific points outlined in the activity directions (4.29). Did the student correctly use the comparison/contrast method in his paper? Did he cite specific examples to prove his statements? Did he first draw up and then follow a well organized outline? Is his reasoning clear? Does the paper cover all the necessary points and stay within the assignment limit? These criteria will help the teacher to properly evaluate this writing assignment. Remember that mechanics are important, but content, too, is vital. Perhaps a separate grade for each category is indicated for this paper.

Additional Learning Activities
Section I Historical Background
    1. Discuss these questions with the class.
       a. What was the economic position of most nonconformists?
       b. What were some positive economic results of the Industrial Revolution?
       c. What were some social and cultural consequences of the Industrial Revolution that many contemporary writers considered destructive?
    2. Divide the class into two debate teams, one group taking the American view of American independence from England, and one group taking the British view. Have the British team read Edmund Burke's *Speech on Moving...for Conciliation with the Colonies*, available at a public library. Both sides should research their positions before the class debate.
    3. Divide the class into several groups (3-7) and have each group choose a periodical listed in LIFEPAC 1207. Each group should research and report the history of its selected periodical.
    4. Suggest that students who are interested research the histories of various Protestant denominations and report their findings.
    5. Have students compare England's Commonwealth and Glorious Revolution to revolutions in France and America.
Section II Puritan Literature of the Seventeenth Century
    1. Milton's character Satan in *Paradise Lost* has fascinated some readers because of his supposed bravery against adversity. Yet Satan's bravery is actually a mixture of revenge and inflexibility. Ask students how Adam in Book XII illustrates true bravery.
    2. Ask students to find examples of psychological realism in Pilgrim's Progress.

3. Rehearse and present a choral reading of sections from Book VII of *Paradise Lost*.
4. Divide the class into groups of two and direct each group to write a short allegory. Have students begin with a doctrine, then with personifications and symbols, and so forth.
5. Have each student select an image from Milton's writings and trace its use through given sections.
6. Have each student write a character sketch of a chosen character in *Pilgrim's Progress*.

Section III Satire from the Literature of Common Sense

1. Discuss these questions with the class.
   a. What method of satire was used in *Gulliver's Travels* to satirize Sir Robert Walpole?
   b. What methods were used to make *Gulliver's Travels* resemble a travel or voyage book?
2. Have students organize their own *Scriblerus Clubs*(?) and ask them to draw up lists of foolish practices to satirize.
3. Have groups of students work collectively on short, fictional travel writing that emphasizes day-to-day detail.
4. Choose talented students to write short satires and to explain their methods.
5. Have students read Pope's Essay on Criticism and ask them to find couplets which illustrate Pope's many uses of heroic couplets.

Section IV Literature of Sensibility

1. Discuss these questions with the class.
   a. How did Samuel Johnson help to shape the values and education of the middle class?
   b. What devices in *The Deserted Village* look back to the Neoclassical period?
   c. What devices in *The Deserted Village* anticipate the new feelings and themes of the nineteenth century?
   d. List the sentimental passages in *The Deserted Village*. How would Pope or Milton have dealt with those same passages?
2. Rehearse and present a choral reading of *The Deserted Village*. Have students note the pitch they must use to emphasize the poem's persuasive purpose.
3. Have students examine a copy of Johnson's *Dictionary of the English Language* (available at a public or college library). Note Johnson's attitudes reflected in his definitions. Students may even want to write entries for their own dictionaries.
4. History majors might enjoy researching the actual number of people who left England to go to America, Canada, or Australia during the later part of the eighteenth century.
5. Students might also research the actual number of poor, rural people clustering in industrialized areas during this period.

Materials Needed for LIFEPAC

Required:

Suggested:
The Holy Bible, King James Version
World Book Dictionary
an approved poetry anthology

Extended Writing Assignment

1. Refer to section 1201 of this handbook for basic grading guidelines. The teacher may wish to review the concepts of evaluating a journal (see Adult check in 1208). As an alternative to a letter grade for a creative writing assignment, consider "satisfactory" or "unsatisfactory" comments, accompanied by lengthy comments to the student, detailing the weaknesses and strengths of the work. Remember that students can be devastated by a remark, even one that may seem inconsequential to the teacher. Therefore, a teacher should weigh words carefully and try to be as precise as possible in pointing out problems and strengths so that students have concrete suggestions to build upon. Give students frequent opportunities to write and to share their writing with class members, if they wish. This kind of encouragement is far better for students than graded assignments; save letter grades for objective tests and for expository writing. Above all, be honest with your students in sharing your comments. Praise them lavishly for truly well written, honestly felt and honestly expressed material, but don't offer false praise. The best incentive you can give your students it to encourage them to read widely, sampling the writings of many writers and finding many approaches to similar problems of living.

2. Read student poems. They should contain at least eight lines with meter and a set rhyme scheme. Remember to evaluate these creative papers in the manner described.

3. Read student poems. They should contain at least fifteen lines of free verse. Remember to evaluate these creative papers in the manner described.

Additional Learning Activities
Section I Reading Fiction and Poetry

1. See if your school or city library has recordings of authors reading their works. Students enjoy hearing poets and writers reading a work currently being studied by the class. This activity may introduce a section or may be used effectively after students have begun the unit.

2. Discuss several short stories with the class. The teacher might open the discussion with immediate student perceptions or with a controversial quote by the writer taken from an interview (use the MLA Bibliography for sources, if available). Then, perhaps proceed with the elements of a short story, working from the simplest (setting, plot, summary, characterization) to the most complex (difficulties, ambiguities of characterization, theme).

3. One way to promote class response and a community feeling is to assign a pair of students (or let two students choose) a short story to teach to the class. The teacher should make the assignment several days in advance so students may prepare thoroughly. They will feel more confident if they feel they can do a good job. This assignment works best if the teacher has first directed discussions for several stories, using a similar format each time so that students can see a workable pattern. Students may use this guideline, preparing questions for class discussion. Have students use in-depth, analytical, thought-provoking questions as well as merely simple recall.

You may also have each pair give a brief quiz to the class; that pair would then be responsible for grading the quiz (objective questions might be best) and for giving you the grades. Not only do the two students preparing the lesson learn cooperation, but the class immediately learns that discussion depends on each person, and that each student will have a turn teaching a short story or poem-so students quickly help each other out. This lesson has great rewards for the time when the teacher returns to directing class discussion, because students realize it is not just the teacher's responsibility; but the entire class is responsible for the lesson proceeding in an interesting manner.

4. Some educational channels of public television provide interviews with famous writers and poets. Students may elect to watch such programs, recommended by the teacher, and then report on one program to the class. Students may wish to combine the television project with more intensive reading of the author's works.

Section II Writing the Short Story

1. Imitation is a time-honored method of instruction, dating back to Aristotle. It may be used in a writing class to teach the concept of style and to foster a student's own personal style. After reading any assigned short story from an anthology, have students isolate, in class discussion, elements of that writer's style: word choice, setting, sentence construction, and whatever else may be appropriate. Next, have students write a one- or two-paragraph imitation of that style. Then after fifteen or twenty minutes, ask students to volunteer their imitations. From time to time, the teacher may inject ideas. Many students will probably be surprised that the teacher attempts the exercise; many teachers, unfortunately, exempt themselves from such experiences, thinking perhaps it is undignified or not worthwhile Students, however, love a good sport and will enjoy the teacher's efforts—whether they be superior or inferior to theirs. Students need to have role models for situations, and by this type of experience, gain true respect for the teacher's writing abilities. Even if the teacher's abilities are not strong in writing, the exercise should still be beneficial. This activity may be adapted to any type of writing experience—from thesis statements to sonnets.

2. If any published writers of fiction live in the area, try to contact them to see if they would be willing to speak to the class. If a writer accepts, have small groups of students serve as a hosting-interviewing committee, making the arrangements for the visit, welcoming the speaker, leading the class discussion (do have the students prepare by reading the author's work and perhaps some published interviews and criticism), then writing thank-you notes and an interview for the school or local newspaper.

3. Send students to the library to look up interviews of their favorite authors. The teacher may, of course, present an approved list to the students for their selection of authors. It may be advisable to screen suggested interviews to ascertain their suitability for the students. Student may give either a brief oral report or a written synopsis of the interview to be handed in to the teacher.

Section III Writing the Poem

1. Refer to the Teacher-Directed Activity for Section II. It may be adapted to poetry, imitating the style, rhyme scheme, and meter pattern of another poet.

2. The teacher may wish to consult John Ciardi's *How Does A Poem Mean*? for specific ideas in discussing poetry.

3. Some poems lend themselves to translation into other forms. Small groups of students may use a poem as the germ (basis) of an original skit, another poem, a song, an original musical composition, or an original painting or sculpture. This activity would also be workable as an Independent Activity for this section, if a teacher should so desire.

4. Students may wish to locate teacher-approved narrative poems. Practice reading them in a natural and interesting manner, then present them to the class.

5. Students may wish to memorize teacher approved poems for class presentation. Letter grades should be discouraged; the goal should be an appreciation of poetry.

6. Students may wish to select a poem (or a collection of poems on a single topic or by a single author), then illustrate it.

Materials Needed for LIFEPAC
    Required:

Suggested:
The Holy Bible, King James Version
World Book Dictionary
Language Arts LIFEPACs 1205 through 1207
World Book Encyclopedia

Extended Writing Assignment

1. For basic grading guidelines, refer to section 1201, Extended Writing Assignment. For this assignment, look for cumulative skills of preceding LIFEPACs. The summary should be in the student's words and should include bibliographical sources at the end of the theme.

2. See the preceding check. For this assignment, see that the student has synthesized material in order to indicate similarities between Romantic artists and poets. Check for logical comparison/contrast form.

3. Look for specific details of comparison/contrast between Tennyson's and Wordsworth's views of the relationship between man and nature. For basic grading guidelines, refer to section 1201 of this handbook.

Additional Learning Activities
Section I Romantic Revolution and Victorian Variety
    1. Use the materials throughout the LIFEPAC as the basis for class discussion (for example, 1.12 and 1.13; 1.15; 1.23 and 1.24; 1.31; 1.048; etc.). The material is too important and too difficult to treat it merely as a completion exercise for your students. Have students complete the material for homework, perhaps, thus preparing themselves for your further discussion of the material.
    2. Divide the class into small groups. Students may research one of the related arts (painting, sculpture, architecture, music, dance, furniture, clothing, cuisine, or theatre) of either the Romantic or the Victorian periods, looking for similarities to those characteristics presented in the LIFEPAC. To see the interrelationship of the arts and of ideas within a given period of time can be helpful to the student. Refer students to the Pelican Guide, Volume 6. The small groups may then assemble posters illustrating their discoveries and share them with the class in a brief oral presentation.
    3. Several public television programs (educational TV) have aired British productions of the Victorian era. With your discretion, students may be encouraged to watch these programs showing life in Victorian England.

Section II Romantic Poets
    1. Use the following assignments for further class discussion: 2.14; 2.17 through 2.20; 2.27 through 2.36; 2.46 through 2.56; 2.62 through 2.64; 2.70 through 2.74; 2.86 through 2.91; 2.92 through 2.93; 2.98 through 2.99, 2.117 through 2.118; and any others that students may find difficult.

2. Students may wish to construct a time line, beginning with the authors and works discussed in this LIFEPAC. The time line could be constructed so that parallel American and continental literature could be added (perhaps by future classes). The teacher might wish to include inventions, important dates, and so forth, in an effort to tie these developments together for students.

3. Sometimes the 1960s have been characterized as a romantic revival. Students may agree or disagree writing a two- or three-page (250 words) theme to be turned in. The Extended Writing Assignment of section 1201 of this handbook contains guidelines for grading. The papers should show cumulative writing skills developed throughout the year.

Section III Victorian Poets

1. Discuss in detail with the class the following activities: 3.6 through 3.8; 3.9; 3.33 through 3.36; 3.57; 3.63; 3.72.; 3.73 through 3.79. Guide the students into thinking more deeply than they may if you merely allow them to fill in the blanks.

2. Using a teacher-approved anthology (perhaps the Norton anthology of Victorian Literature), have students explore works by other writers of the period. They may wish to read essays (Ruskin, Arnold, or Carlyle), novels (Brontës, Eliot, Thackeray, Meredith, or Hardy), or more poetry.

3. Students may give oral or written book reports on teacher approved biographies of prominent romantics or Victorians.

Materials Needed for LIFEPAC

Required:

Suggested:
The Holy Bible, King James Version
World Book Dictionary
an approved literature anthology

Extended Writing Assignment

1. Check the three-paragraph essay (1.65) for logic, coherence, and unity. Check the essay using the basic grading guidelines in section 1201 of this handbook. The skills are cumulative, so this essay should be better written than those essays produced earlier in the year.

2. Since the short story is indeed a creative effort, student's efforts will vary greatly. Remember that creativity may be fostered or be crushed by the teacher's comments. The teacher might choose to substitute comments or a general "satisfactory" or "unsatisfactory" rating for letter grades. See Extended Writing Assignment, section 1208 for guidelines in evaluating creative writing. Be certain, however, that all the elements of the short story have been included. Students may wish to share their stories with the class.

3. Read the student's poem (1.81). Refer to Extended Writing Assignment, section 1208 of this handbook for guidelines about assigning letter grades to creative writing.

Additional Learning Activities
Section I Language
1. The teacher may divide the class into groups of five. The teacher then assigns the entire class one prefix, suffix, or root. The groups should write down as many words as possible within a certain time limit. The group with the most correct words wins. Bonus points may be given for foreign words, words with more than one syllable, and so forth. The class may devise its own rules for bonus points.
2. Divide the class into two teams. Each team should send a representative to the board to play Hangman's Bluff using words with prefixes or suffixes from the LIFEPAC.
3. Divide the class into three groups. Have group leaders draw a word from a container; the rest of the group should be lined up behind the leader. The leader mimes the word, until the word is guessed by his group; all three groups will be simultaneously involved. The first group to guess all members' mimes wins.
4. Have students listen to instrumental music (classical such as *Water Music, Danse Macabre, Grand Canyon Suite, Sorcerer's Apprentice, Pictures at an Exhibition*, a Strauss Waltz, or jazz such as Chuck Mangione's *Feels So Good, Bellavia*, or *Children of Sanchez*, John Klemmer's *Barefoot Ballet*, or Maynard Ferguson's *Conquistador*). Students may use earphones if available. Students should then write a poem or descriptive prose suggested by the mood of the music. Students may wish to listen to the recordings several times before and during the composition. These poems may be shared with the class, after playing the music.

Section II English Literature: Medieval and Renaissance
1. Students may enjoy planning and participating in a Medieval or Renaissance Fair with appropriate games, food, and entertainment. In some cities, a society exists to explore anachronistic activities; these members often lecture to classes as well as provide jousting tournaments. Posters of costumes, filmstrips, and soundtracks taping Elizabethan music may be used.

2. Divide the class into five groups. Assign each group an act from *Hamlet* Each group, one day in class, will translate the Elizabethan verse into contemporary prose, shortening the action of the script but retaining the essential action and the flavor of the act as much as possible. On the second day, the groups may have about ten minutes each to present each act in sequence. If there is time at the end of class, the students may discuss the strengths and weaknesses of their presentations.

3. Students interested in cooking may like to research appropriate recipes, preparing a medieval or Renaissance banquet or simply a dessert to share with the class.

4. If your students have access to cassette tapes of Shakespeare's plays, they may like to check them out for individual listening projects and enjoyment.

5. If a Shakespearean acting company visits your area, students may be encouraged to attend performances, then discuss the plays with you and other class members.

Section III English Literature: Restoration, Romantics, and Victorians

1. Choose a topic (such as, higher taxes, the crime rate, political corruption) and discuss effective ways this topic could be satirized. Caution against involving specific personalities or highly controversial subjects.

2. After the preceding class discussion students may want to form groups to satirize problem areas in society. Students may write their satires or present a satirical skit.

3. A group of students may wish to present a slide or slide-tape show to the class, basing their work upon one of the writers reviewed in this LIFEPAC. After researching the writer's life (suggest they start with an encyclopedia or the *Dictionary of National Biographies*, then proceed to more specialized books), students may begin assembling data about the writer's life. Many schools have photographic labs and can take slides directly from books greatly simplifying the task of locating materials.

4. Students who enjoy drawing may like to sketch a scene suggested by their reading of one of the poems in the review LIFEPAC. Other possibilities include composing a mood piece complementary to one of the poems, creating a short skit, pantomime, or reading based on an idea from the poems, or creating a sculpture or painting derived imaginatively from the poems. Students may suggest other related ideas; certainly the interrelationship of the arts is an attitude to be fostered, appreciated, and enjoyed.

ALTERNATE

TESTS

Reproducible Tests
for use with the Language Arts
1200 Teacher's Guide

Name _____

Match these items (each answer, 2 points).

1. _____ *trans-*

2. _____ *cosmos*

3. _____ *-ist*

4. _____ *logos*

5. _____ *-itis*

6. _____ *ante-*

7. _____ *anti-*

8. _____ *-ism*

9. _____ *ex-*

10. _____ *per-*

a. doctrine or belief

b. inflammation

c. against

d. across

e. out of, formerly

f. one who believes

g. word, reason, study

h. through, thoroughly

i. before

j. world, world system

k. quality or condition

Write *true* or *false* (each answer, 1 point).

11. _____ Many words can be formed from one root by the addition of common prefixes and suffixes.

12. _____ The prefix *hypo-* means *above* or *very*.

13. _____ Analytical prose is the most common type of everyday communication.

14. _____ Every paragraph should display unity and coherence.

15. _____ A topic sentence states the main idea of a paragraph.

16. _____ Adding interesting comments to your paragraphs, even if they are not directly related to the topic sentence, adds desirable variety and spice to your writing and keeps the reader awake.

17. _____ An outline is an efficient way to improve your writing because it forces you to be logical and analytical.

18. _____ A transition works as a supplementary topic sentence.

19. _____ A pronoun must agree with its antecedent in person, number, and gender.

20. _____ Shifting the tense from past to future and present and back to past insures that your reader will stay alert and make sense out of your writing.

Write the letter of the correct answer on the line (each answer, 2 points).

21. A word which means *a society ruled by the father* is _____.

    a. *patrician*   c. *patricide*
    b. *patriarchy*   d. *patrimony*

22. The type of writing most often required of college students is _____.

    a. descriptive   c. expository
    b. analytical   d. argumentative

23. One of the following words is *not* a transition: _____.

    a. furthermore   c. finally
    b. another point to consider   d. under

24. Correct interior punctuation of the following sentence, "It's not a question of who's going to throw the first stone it's a question of who's going to start building with it," would be _____.

    a. stone; it's   c. stone, but it's
    b. stone. It's   d. a, b, and c

25. An introductory paragraph should do all of the following *except:* _____.

    a. apologize for the choice of subject
    b. introduce the subject
    c. gain the reader's attention
    d. state the thesis in the last sentence of the introduction

Complete these statements (each answer, 3 points).

26. The special vocabulary of a particular field of interest is called

    a. _____ or b. _____ .

27. A *height name,* a word made from the initial capital letters of the name

    of a group or project (for example OPEC) is called a(n) _____

    _____ .

28. Balancing nouns with nouns, infinitives with infinitives, and prepositional

    phrases with prepositional phrases results in elements called _____

    _____ .

29. The level of diction derived from a Latin term meaning *conversation,* a

    level inappropriate for most themes, is called _____ .

30. A tool that is helpful in finding precise synonyms and antonyms is

    called a(n) _____ .

51 / 64

Name _____

Complete these statements (each answer, 3 points).

1. Sentences must have a. _____ or b. _____
   to indicate the subject.

2. Tangible objects are called _____ nouns.

3. Adjectives and adverbs are _____ .

4. In the following sentence, "He drives carelessly," the word *carelessly*

   is used as a(n) _____ .

5. Most linguists agree on _____ basic sentence patterns
   for the English language.

6. The three verbal phrases are a. _____ , b. _____ ,

   and c. _____ .

7. A participle has _____ forms.

8. A dependent clause has a(n) a. _____ and a(n)

   b. _____ but cannot represent a complete thought by
   itself.

Answer *true* or *false* (each answer, 1 point).

9. _____ Thought processes, ideas, or other intangible things are
   called concrete nouns.

10. _____ An adjective can be used after a linking verb as a subject
    complement.

11. _____ The predicate of the sentence is the verb or verb phrase.

12. _____ The expletive is an introductory word followed by the adjective.

13. _____ To subordinate an idea, phrase, or clause you must make it
    depend upon a main clause or complete sentence.

14. _____ Conjunctions and prepositions can be interchanged.

15. _____ In the sentence, "My people hath been lost sheep," the word
    lost is a past participle.

16. _____ The gerund, a verb form that ends only in *-ing*, is used as
    an adverb.

17. _____ Infinitives can be used as nouns, as adjectives, or as adverbs.

18. _____ The nominative absolute is a phrase consisting of a noun or
    noun substitute followed by a participle and complements or
    modifiers.

57

List these items (each answer, 3 points).

19. three categories of pronouns

     a. _____

     b. _____

     c. _____

20. the six tenses in the English language

     a. _____   d. _____

     b. _____   e. _____

     c. _____   f. _____

21. four of the seven basic sentence patterns

     a. _____   c. _____

     b. _____   d. _____

22. four examples of relative pronouns

     a. _____   c. _____

     b. _____   d. _____

Write the basic pattern of each sentence on the line (each answer, 2 points).

23. _____ Charlie slept soundly until morning.

24. _____ She has given Carole her assignment for tomorrow.

25. _____ March 10 is my mother's birthday.

26. _____ My brother injured his leg while playing tennis.

27. _____ That book is interesting and informative.

86 / 107

Date _____

Score _____

Name _____

Match these items (each answer, 2 points).

1. _____ illustration

2. _____ dictionary

3. _____ magazine

4. _____ visual skill

5. _____ supporting details

6. _____ Library of Congress system

7. _____ opinion

8. _____ key sentence

9. _____ fact

10. _____ card catalogue

a. something that exists or is true

b. statement of the main idea in a paragraph

c. alphabetical listing of words and information

d. facts, names, and dates in a piece of writing

e. periodical containing miscellaneous material

f. table of contents

g. expertise in seeing words accurately

h. an anecdote, story, example, or incident to illustrate a point

i. individual response; not provable

j. used by most college libraries for cataloguing

k. alphabetical listing of books in a library

Write *true* or *false* (each answer, 1 point).

11. _____ Melchizedek differed greatly from the King of Sodom.

12. _____ *The Oxford English Dictionary* is of historical value.

13. _____ Drawing conclusions is making implications.

14. _____ Note taking is a waste of valuable time.

15. _____ Moving the lips while reading does not slow the reading.

16. _____ Card catalogues are divided into author, title, and subject.

17. _____ The *Readers' Guide* does not handle enough magazine entries to be of great consequence.

18. _____ A service directory lists church services.

19. _____ Those who read know more than those who never read.

20. _____ A process analysis paragraph instructs one how to do something.

Complete these statements (each answer, 3 points).

21. Rapid locating of specific information is called _____ .

22. ISBN is the abbreviation for _____ .

23. An alphabetical recording of names is a _____ .

24. A card for recording research information is called a _____ .

25. Most high school libraries in this country use the _____ _____ system for listing books.

26. Using another's words in a paper without giving that original author credit is _____ .

27. An alphabetical listing of items in a book or newspaper is a(n) _____ .

28. A listing of magazine articles can be found in the _____ .

29. The "how to" kind of writing is termed _____ .

30. A conclusion drawn from suggested ideas is a(n) _____ .

31. The main idea of a paragraph is usually found in the _____ .

32. A twelve-volume dictionary dealing with the history of the English language is the _____ .

33. The three types of cards found in a card catalogue are a. _____ , b. _____ , and c. _____ .

34. Comparison/contrast is one of the categories of _____ writing.

Write the letter of the correct answer on the line (each answer, 2 points).

35. Expository writing using phrases like *either/or* or *similarity/difference* falls into the _____ pattern.

    a. descriptive   c. comparison-contrast
    b. definition   d. illustrative

36. Supporting details in a well-written paragraph should be based on _____ .

    a. opinion   c. ideas
    b. fact   d. beliefs

37. Dictionaries, card catalogues, and indexes are all classified as _____.

    a. research tools
    b. literary criticism

    c. fiction
    d. sources

38. The order of listing in most directories is _____.

    a. historical
    b. realistic

    c. miscellaneous
    d. alphabetical

39. Donald E. Smith developed a four-part pattern to increase _____ skills.

    a. writing
    b. listening

    c. research
    d. reading

40. Newspaper indexes are usually found _____.

    a. in the second section
    b. on the back page

    c. on the front page
    d. in the classified section

```
 72 /
    / 90
```

Date _____

Score _____

Name _____

Write *true* or *false* (each answer, 1 point).

1. _____ Webster compiled the first dictionary in the United States.

2. _____ Structural linguistics deal with phonemes and morphemes.

3. _____ Darwin published *The Origin of Species* in the twentieth century.

4. _____ Socrates was the first person to separate parts of speech.

5. _____ The purpose of grammar is to organize language into logical divisions.

6. _____ The originator of transformational grammar was Noam Chomsky.

7. _____ The language of infants is classified as casual.

8. _____ Morphology is the branch of grammar dealing with the forms of words.

9. _____ Students use formal language among their peers.

10. _____ English grammars are based on Greek roots.

Match these items (each answer, 2 points).

11. _____ morphology
12. _____ case
13. _____ fallacy
14. _____ syntax
15. _____ phonology
16. _____ paradigm
17. _____ angular gyrus
18. _____ I. A. Richards
19. _____ S. I. Hayakawa
20. _____ Koiné Greek
21. _____ Charles Fries
22. _____ morpheme

a. study of word sounds and pronunciation
b. branch of grammar dealing with arrangement of words and phrases in a sentence
c. a study of word forms
d. a pattern or example
e. false idea or mistaken belief
f. a form of a noun or pronoun
g. a structural linguist
h. nerve center of the brain
i. semantics and literary criticism
j. a term of generative grammar
k. greatly advanced study of general semantics
l. common Greek
m. smallest unit of meaning in a word

Complete these statements (each answer, 3 points).

23. Both the Peruvian Indians and Scandinavians believed language to be a

    gift from their _____ .

24. English developed from a _____ language.

25. The language of the New Testament is _____ .

26. The famous conqueror who introduced Greek culture to Persia, Egypt,

    and India was _____ .

27. The first attempts to devise a grammar for the English language began

    during the _____ .

28. Latin nouns and pronouns have a. _____ number of cases

    while English has b. _____ .

29. Traditional grammar deals basically with _____
    English.

30. A sentence consisting of a noun and verb phrase in its simplest form

    is a _____ .

31. The term *semantics* is derived from a word in the _____
    language.

Define these terms (each answer, 4 points).

32. connotation _____

    _____

33. lateralization _____

    _____

34. context _____

    _____

<table>
<tr><td>61</td></tr>
<tr><td>76</td></tr>
</table>

Date _____

Score _____

Name _____

Write the letter of the correct answer on the line (each answer, 2 points).

1. The monster Beowulf fought was _____.

   a. Chaucer   c. Chaunticleer
   b. Grendel   d. William the conqueror

2. A religious martyr of the Middle Ages was _____.

   a. Becket   c. Arthur
   b. Beowulf   d. Chaucer

3. The people of Southern Sweden are called _____.

   a. Britons   c. Bretons
   b. Celts   d. Geats

4. The Danish king in *Beowulf* was _____.

   a. Hrothgar   c. Becket
   b. Grendel   d. Arthur

5. The head of a convent in *Canterbury Tales* is called the _____.

   a. Nun   c. Prioress
   b. Priest   d. Franklin

6. Chaunticleer is a _____.

   a. king   c. dragon
   b. rooster   d. monster

7. The Norman who invaded and conquered England was_____.

   a. Arthur   c. William
   b. Edward   d. James

8. Pearl is a girl representing _____.

   a. love   c. truth
   b. purity   d. religion

9. *Wyrd* is another word for _____.

   a. fate   c. battle
   b. death   d. monster

10. A famous Anglo-Saxon historian was _____.

    a. Edward the Confessor   c. Geoffrey Chaucer
    b. William the Conqueror   d. Venerable Bede

Match these items (each answer, 2 points).

11. _____ kennings

12. _____ final *e*

13. _____ 1066 A.D.

14. _____ Chaucer

15. _____ longbow

16. _____ Southeast Midland

17. _____ landowner

18. _____ bronze

19. _____ Magna Carta

20. _____ the dragon

21. _____ The Black Death

22. _____ The Crusades

a. Battle of Hastings

b. breakthrough in warfare of middle ages

c. device of Anglo-Saxon poetry

d. a Franklin

e. neutral vowel in Middle English

f. signed by King John

g. London dialect from which English developed

h. bubonic plague

i. "The Nun's Priest's Tale"

j. metal for weapons in early Briton

k. wars to recapture the Holy Land

l. Beowulf's last foe

m. Thomas à Becket

Write *true* or *false* (each answer, 1 point).

23. _____ Much is known about the very early people of the British Isles.

24. _____ The Celts conquered England in 1066.

25. _____ The year 597 marks the beginnings of English history.

26. _____ Venerable Bede is the father of English history.

27. _____ Alfred the Great began the *Anglo-Saxon Chronicles*.

28. _____ *Beowulf* is a long, narrative poem divided into two main sections.

29. _____ "The Wanderer" is an English epic.

30. _____ "The Seafarer" is a poetic description of the remains of a Roman city in England.

31. _____ A ballad can be historical or nonhistorical.

32. _____ "Sir Orfeo" is a famous Breton lay.

Complete these statements (each answer, 3 points).

33. A formal poem that is a poet's meditation about a serious subject is a(n) _____ .

34. Pithy, succinct sayings that are maxims in verse form are called

    _____ .

35. In eleventh-century England William the Conqueror compiled a list of all property holdings that was called the _____ .

36. Three of the types of literature of the twelfth century were

    a. _____ , b. _____ ,

    and c. _____ .

37. The growth of towns and the development of the middle class are two factors contributing to the decline of _____ in the fourteenth century.

38. *Canterbury Tales* not only pictured life in fourteenth-century England but also presented people from all _____ of English society.

39. The opening section of the *Canterbury Tales* that introduces the characters is called the _____ .

40. One of the finest elegies in the English language is the fourteenth-century dream-vision poem called _____ .

41. *Sir Gawain and the Green Knight* is a fourteenth-century romance set in the time of _____ .

42. In Chaucer's *Canterbury Tales* the Parson and the Plowman represent

    a. _____ and b. _____ .

74 / 93

Date _____

Score _____

Name _____

Answer *true* or *false* (each answer, 1 point).

1. _____ Elizabethan theater used no costumes.

2. _____ Tragedy deals with a light subject.

3. _____ There are many differences between Elizabethan theater and modern drama.

4. _____ The language of Shakespeare's plays is Medieval English.

5. _____ The sonnet is a specialized type of lyric poetry.

6. _____ A miracle play is based on the lives of the saints.

7. _____ A morality play is a dramatic allegory.

8. _____ The origins of English drama are the church plays of the Renaissance.

9. _____ The subjects of mystery plays are abstractions.

10. _____ The King James Version of the Bible was written in the early 1600's.

Match these items (each answer, 2 points).

11. _____ image

12. _____ Richard Tottel

13. _____ concrete

14. _____ sonnet

15. _____ Sir Philip Sidney

16. _____ *The Faerie Queen*

17. _____ archaic

18. _____ the "Dark Lady"

19. _____ epistle

20. _____ "The Prodigal Son"

21. _____ Sir Francis Bacon

22. _____ John Heywood

a. something that can be perceived by the senses

b. wrote Italian sonnets

c. belonging to an earlier period, outdated

d. a word picture

e. means *little song* in Italian

f. first collection of songs and lyrics in England

g. Edmund Spenser

h. Elizabethan Age

i. subject of Shakespeare's sonnets

j. a parable

k. a letter

l. famous writer of interludes

m. first English essayist

Write the letter for the correct answer on the line (each answer, 2 points).

23. The turning point of a play is its _____.

    a. exposition
    b. climax
    c. resolution
    d. action

24. The validity of a critical essay is determined by its _____.

    a. evidence
    b. construction
    c. thesis
    d. conclusion

25. The hero of a tragedy fails and falls because of his _____.

    a. dialogue
    b. action
    c. tragic flaw
    d. personality

26. The mystery plays were based on _____.

    a. scripture
    b. poetry
    c. legend
    d. history

27. The time and place of a play is its _____.

    a. character
    b. stage directions
    c. dialogue
    d. setting

28. Shakespeare's greatest plays were performed first in _____.

    a. the court
    b. courtyards of inns
    c. churches
    d. the Globe theater

29. After the age of Elizabethan drama, the theaters were closed by _____.

    a. the king
    b. the Catholic Church
    c. the Puritans
    d. Parliament

30. Expressions or ideas that have become trite are _____.

    a. clichés
    b. sonnets
    c. dialogue
    d. images

31. *Hamlet* is classified as a _____.

    a. comedy
    b. tragedy
    c. mystery play
    d. allegory

32. The setting of Shakespeare's *Hamlet* is _____.

    a. England
    b. Scotland
    c. Denmark
    d. Ireland

Complete these statements (each answer, 3 points).

33. Shakespeare's plays can be classified into the three broad categories

    of a. _____ , b. _____ , and c. _____ .

34. A writer giving human characteristics to an inanimate object is

    _____ .

35. The struggle between opposing forces in a play is the _____ .

36. The climax of a play is followed by the _____ .

37. The two types of conflict that can exist in any play are a. _____

    _____ and b. _____ .

38. The most famous morality play is probably _____ .

39. A humorous scene inserted in a play to provide emotional relaxation

    is classified as _____ .

40. Criticism is primarily a process of a. _____ ,

    b. _____ , and c. _____ .

41. Answering the question, "What does the writer say to me?" is called

    _____ .

42. The Greek root of the word *criticism* means _____ .

```
+-----+
| 79 /|
|  / |
| /99 |
+-----+
```

Date _____

Score _____

Language Arts 1207 Alternate Test

Name _____

Answer *true* or *false* (each answer, 1 point).

1. _____ In *The Deserted Village*, the villagers are driven from their homes because the Enclosure Acts have enabled a wealthy landowner to buy the public property.

2. _____ In that same poem, the poet says that the villagers will either go to America or to crowded, corrupted charity homes.

3. _____ In *Gulliver's Travels*, the king of Brobdingnag observes that most men are morally qualified for their careers.

4. _____ Goldsmith wrote a novel entitled *The Vicar of Wakefield*, about a parson's family.

5. _____ At the end of *The Deserted Village*, Poetry leaves with the rural virtues and the displaced villagers because people left in England are too corrupted by wealth to appreciate art.

6. _____ The Puritans felt that the Anglican Church was corrupted.

7. _____ Oliver Goldsmith believed that extreme wealth is destructive.

8. _____ Oliver Goldsmith wrote very few periodical essays.

9. _____ In *The Deserted Village*, Goldsmith insults the sentimental village preacher.

10. _____ Samuel Johnson wrote periodical essays in numerous newspapers.

Match these items (each answer, 2 points).

11. _____ a cause for which Swift wrote

12. _____ Tory party

13. _____ subject of *The Deserted Village*

14. _____ *Gulliver's Travels*

15. _____ "labouring swain" is an example

16. _____ Johnson believed literature should appeal mainly to this person

17. _____ political events of second half of the eighteenth century

18. _____ published by Johnson

19. _____ published by Goldsmith

20. _____ simile

a. a political satire
b. William III's Whig wars
c. scholar
d. destruction of village life
e. common man
f. the devaluation of Irish coins
g. *The Vicar of Wakefield*
h. Swift's, Johnson's, Goldsmith's political party
i. poetic diction
j. *A Dictionary of the English Language*
k. growing British Empire
l. a comparison using *like* or *as*
m. metaphor
n. Whig

Write the letter of the correct answer on the line (each answer, 2 points).

21. In "On the Morning of Christ's Nativity," what did Christ forsake and what did He choose? _____

    a. He left Heaven to live in darkness as a mortal.
    b. He left the "Darksome earth" to join His Father.
    c. He left God's side to be alone in the wilderness.
    d. He left Mary's side to turn water into wine.

22. In "On His Blindness," Milton regrets _____.

    a. that God is so unfair
    b. that he is in prison
    c. that he is blind
    d. that his blindness restricts his work

23. The repetition of initial consonants is _____.

    a. satire   c. alliteration
    b. personification   d. simile

24. Verse having units of two rhyming lines with five iambic feet in each line is written in _____.

    a. allegory   c. sonnets
    b. heroic couplets   d. didactic couplets

25. To give something human characteristics is to _____ it.

    a. satirize   c. address
    b. personify   d. condemn

26. A story in which things represent parts of a doctrine or theme is _____.

    a. a satire   c. an allegory
    b. a personification   d. a sonnet

27. A poem with fourteen lines, either Italian or English, is _____.

    a. a satire   c. an allegory
    b. a heroic couplet   d. a sonnet

28. A type of literature that ridicules something to correct behavior is _____.

    a. a satire   c. an allegory
    b. a personification   d. a sonnet

Complete these statements (each answer, 3 points).

29. Periodicals and the novel became more popular as the more powerful

    _____ class began to read.

30. Milton was imprisoned because of his previous position in the _____

    _____ .

31. Charles II was _____ to the throne in 1660.

32. When public land was_____for private estates, many
    of the rural poor were driven away.

33. John Bunyan studied _____ after the civil war.

34. The Commonwealth and the Industrial Revolution helped to create a

    _____ .

35. The poet takes the loss of *The Deserted Village* personally because

    _____ .

Answer these questions (each answer, 5 points).

36. How are Bunyan's characters in *Pilgrim's Progress* more than just

    symbols? _____

    _____

37. What is one country or group of people that Swift used in *Gulliver's Travels* to satirize English society? _____

_____

38. In *Pilgrim's Progress* what does the character Christian represent?

_____

_____

66 / 82

Date _____

Score _____

Language Arts 1208 Alternate Test

Name _____

Match these items (each answer, 2 points).

1. _____ plot

2. _____ crisis

3. _____ denouement

4. _____ climax

5. _____ characterization

6. _____ setting

7. _____ protagonist

8. _____ metaphor

9. _____ simile

10. _____ hyperbole

a. high point of action

b. background of time, place, and mood

c. main character

d. story line, action

e. exaggeration, overstatement

f. underlying concept

g. indirect comparison

h. imaginary people made realistic

i. turning point of action

j. direct comparison

k. resolution

Write *true* or *false* (each answer, 1 point).

11. _____ An example of iambic meter would be the word *carpenter*.

12. _____ Onomatopoeia is an element of the short story, named for Edgar Allen Poe, the father of the short story.

13. _____ Elizabeth Barrett Browning is best known for her sonnets.

14. _____ The word that suggests truths and experiences are common to people throughout the world, throughout the ages, is *microcosmic*.

15. _____ A plot is the action framework of a story.

16. _____ *Personification* means the repetition of initial consonant sounds

17. _____ Anything that can be seen, heard, smelled, tasted, or felt is a potential poetic image.

18. _____ The theme of a story is seldom directly stated and must therefore be inferred by the reader from the elements of the story.

19. _____ Poetry must have meter and rhyme in order to be distinguished from prose.

20. _____ Once a poet has established a set meter or rhyme pattern within a poem, he must continue using that pattern throughout the poem to maintain unity.

Write the letter of the correct answer on the line (each answer, 2 points).

21. One of the following terms is *not* a figure of speech: _____ .

    a. metaphor   c. metonymy
    b. irony   d. clerihew

22. "Balloon" and "lagoon" are examples of _____ rhyme.

    a. true   c. alliterative
    b. slant   d. feminine

23. An example of slant rhyme that includes consonance is _____ .

    a. took - look   c. look - luck
    b. look - book   d. look - duck

24. "When fishes flew and forests walked," is an example of _____ .

    a. simile   c. assonance
    b. understatement   d. personification

25. "Ars Poetica" was written by _____ .

    a. Robert Burns   c. Archibald MacLeish
    b. G. K. Chesterton d. Williams Wordsworth

Complete these statements (each answer, 3 points).

26. The crisis, or turning point, of the story is followed by the a. _____

    _____ and then the b. _____ .

27. A character who is static and unchanging, not fully developed, is called

    a a. _____ character as opposed to a dynamic, changing,

    b. _____ character.

28. An element of a short story, novel, or drama that helps establish mood,

    atmosphere, or time is called the _____ .

29. A character drawn from many people and possessing traits of various

    people is called a _____ character.

30. That concept or meaning underlying a fictional work or poem is called

    _____ .

49 / 61

Date _____

Score _____

Language Arts 1209 Alternate Test

Match these items (each answer, 2 points).

1. _____ noble savage

2. _____ Coleridge

3. _____ Dickens

4. _____ Byron

5. _____ Wordsworth

6. _____ Brontë sisters

7. _____ Shelley

8. _____ Thackeray

9. _____ Keats

10. _____ Eliot

a. *Prometheus Unbound,*
   "Ode to the West Wind," "Ozymandias"

b. *Vanity Fair*

c. *Wuthering Heights, Jane Eyre*

d. "Ode on a Grecian Urn," "On First
   Looking into Chapman's Homer,"
   "When I Have Fears"

e. *Silas Marner, Adam Bede, The Mill
   on the Floss*

f. those who lived close to nature,
   were uncorrupted by society, and
   therefore admirable

g. *Childe Harold's Pilgrimage, Don Juan*

h. "the spontaneous overflow of
   powerful emotions . . . recollected
   in tranquility"

i. *Rime of the Ancient Mariner,*
   "Kubla Khan," *Biographia Literaria*

j. "The Emperor of Ice Cream,"
   Paterson

k. *Hard Times, Great Expectations,
   A Tale of Two Cities*

Write *true* or *false* (each answer, 1 point).

11. _____ The romantic revolution in England occurred between 1708 and
1837.

12. _____ The Victorian age of England is named after the queen who
ruled from 1837 to 1901.

13. _____ Romanticism was essentially a reaction against the eighteenth
century's neo-classical emphasis on reason, rules, and
restraint.

14. _____ The American Revolution, the French Revolution, and the Industrial Revolution all led to the atmosphere that encouraged
Romanticism.

15. _____ The Industrial Revolution marked the change of England from an
urban, industrial society into a rural, agricultural one.

16. _____ The 1832 Reform Bill extended the franchise, or right to vote, to all native-born Englishmen.

17. _____ The neoclassicists viewed man as a being who existed within certain boundaries; the romanticists saw man as capable of limitless achievements.

18. _____ Most Victorian writers looked to the past hoping to cure society's problems through history.

19. _____ Victorian conduct was based on the virtues of self-reliance, industriousness, temperance, piety, propriety, and moral simplicity.

20. _____ In "It Is A Beauteous Evening, Calm and Free," Wordsworth speaks to his son, whom he teasingly called "Childe Harold."

Write the letter of the correct answer on the line (each answer, 2 points).

21. The *Lyrical Ballads* were first published in _____.

   a. 1776   c. 1880
   b. 1798   d. 1832

22. The author of the first Preface to *Lyrical Ballads* is _____.

   a. William Wordsworth   c. both men
   b. Samuel Coleridge   d. neither man

23. According to the Romantic theory, a poet creates a poem by _____.

   a. following certain rules of writing
   b. being as objective as possible
   c. waiting for inspiration
   d. meditating on an experience

24. Romantic poetry is sometimes called _____ poetry.

   a. objective   c. immature
   b. nature   d. sensationalist

25. "Tintern Abbey" was written by _____.

   a. Wordsworth   c. Shelley
   b. Coleridge   d. Ruskin

Complete these statements (each answer, 3 points).

26. Opposing the philosophy of greed and materialism so widespread in England during the 1830's, three Anglicans endeavored to restore the Church to a position of spiritual leadership, resulting in a drive

   called the _____ .

27. The line, "'Beauty is truth, truth beauty'—that is all/ye know on
     earth, and ye need to know," comes from a. _____
     _____ , a poem by b. _____ .

28. Five qualities of the Byronic hero include a. _____ ,
     b. _____ , c. _____ ,
     d. _____ , and e. _____ .

29. Characteristics of romanticism include an emphasis upon a. _____ ,
     b. _____ , c. _____ ,
     d. _____ , and e. _____ .

30. The poet who is known for his use of "sprung rhythm" is _____
     _____ .

31. The poet who developed the dramatic monologue is _____
     _____ .

32. The spokesman for the Victorian age is often considered to be
     _____ .

70
88

Date _____

Score _____

Name _____

Match these items (each answer, 2 points).

1. _____ John Bunyan   a. *Canterbury Tales*

2. _____ Robert Browning   b. "God's Grandeur"

3. _____ Charles Dickens   c. "Kubla Khan"

4. _____ Geoffrey Chaucer   d. *Pilgrim's Progress*

5. _____ John Milton   e. "When I Have Fears"

6. _____ Gerard Manley Hopkins   f. "My Last Duchess"

7. _____ George Gordon, Lord   g. *Gulliver's Travels*
             Byron
                                  h. "Tintern Abbey"

8. _____ Samuel Coleridge
                                  i. *Great Expectations*

9. _____ John Keats
                                  j. *Paradise Lost*

10. _____ William Wordsworth
                                  k. *Don Juan*

Write *true* or *false* (each answer, 1 point).

11. _____ The topic sentence of a paragraph is a general statement
              that summarizes the contents of the paragraph.

12. _____ Jonathan Swift wrote *Gulliver's Travels*.

13. _____ Shelley's life was contrary to the ideas he explored in his
              poetry.

14. _____ *The Pearl* is a fifteenth-century elegy containing a dream
              vision.

15. _____ The climax of *Hamlet* is Ophelia's death.

16. _____ All sonnets have fourteen lines.

17. _____ Shakespeare was born in London in 1564.

18. _____ The main support for a critic's opinion should be detailed
              evidence from the text.

19. _____ The first step in writing a critical essay is to be very
              familiar with the text.

20. _____ The philosophy of romanticism was a concern for the rights
              and dignity of the individual.

Write the letter of the correct answer on the line (each answer, 2 points).

21. The Victorian era contrasted _____ .

    a. prosperity and poverty
    b. industrialization and benefits of the past
    c. scientific theory and religious beliefs
    d. revolution and the *status quo*

22. The first serious work of the romantic movement was a collection of poems called _____ .

    a. *Pilgrimage* by Samuel Purcha
    b. *Gulliver's Travels* by Jonathan Swift
    c. *Lyric Ballads* by William Wordsworth
    d. *Rime of the Ancient Mariner* by Samuel Coleridge

23. A poet of the Victorian era was _____ .

    a. Mary Ann Evans (George Eliot)
    b. Charlotte Brontë
    c. Elizabeth Barrett Browning
    d. Christabel Lee

24. Chaucer's holy blissful martyr was _____ .

    a. Joan of Arc   c. Pertelote
    b. Thomas à Becket   d. John Donne

25. The monster slain by Beowulf was _____ .

    a. Chaunticleer   c. Grendel
    b. Wiglaf   d. Wealtheow

Complete these statements (each answer, 3 points).

26. The character in *Hamlet* who is best characterized as shrewd and concerned about outward appearances is _____ .

27. Hamlet's tragic flaw is his _____ .

28. A repetition of initial consonant sounds is called _____

    _____ .

29. The rhythm pattern of a sonnet is _____ .

30. Four types of point of view in a novel or short story include

    a. _____ , b. _____ ,

    c. _____ , and d. _____ .

31. Three kinds of grammar that are studied today are a. _____ ,

    b. _____ , and c. _____ .

32. Three examples of figurative language (figures of speech) include

    a. _____ , b. _____ ,

    and c. _____ .

33. Poetry that has no rhyme or definite rhythm is _____ .

34. Five characteristics of romantic poetry include a. _____ ,

    b. _____ , c. _____ ,

    d. _____ , and e. _____ .

35. The rhyme scheme used by Shelley in which first and third lines rhyme and the final sound of the second line establishes the rhyme for the first and third lines of the following stanza is called

    _____ .

$$\frac{82}{103}$$

Date _____

Score _____

ANSWER KEYS

1.1   Examples:
       predict
       abdicate
       edict
       indicate
       indicative
       addiction

1.2   Examples:
       irrevocable
       revoke
       vocation
       advocate

1.3   Examples:
       inventor
       prevention
       adventure
       convene
       advent

1.4   Examples:
       convertible
       subversive
       invert
       extrovert
       introvert
       pervert

1.5 - 1.8 Hint:
       Check the meaning of the words in
       a dictionary. Be sure complete
       sentences are used.

1.5   Example:
       Your diction is improving.

1.6   Example:
       The rule made for employees is
       irrevocable.

1.7   Example:
       The Advent season signals the com-
       ing of Jesus Christ as Saviour.

1.8   Example:
       That literature is subversive in
       content.

1.9   Examples:
       reduce
       reduction
       produce
       introduce
       induce

1.10   Examples:
       aspect
       inspect
       speculation
       inspector
       respectful
       spectacle

1.11   Examples:
       attainable
       detention
       intend
       pretend
       extend

1.12   Example:
       intermission
       admission
       omission
       remit
       submission

1.13   to turn away

1.14   charitable works

1.15   before the Civil War

1.16   a. Cain
       b. Abel

1.17   king

1.18   to do thoroughly

1.19   eulogy

1.20   is without God

1.21   a cutting out of a person's money

1.22   neurology, neuritis

1.23   body

1.24   theology

1.25   courageous

1.26   beautiful

1.27 spirit of the body

1.28 Examples:
a. inhuman
b. indispensable
c. inadmissible

1.29 One who turns toward another (with hostility)

1.30 Examples:
a. astrologer
b. astronaut
c. astronomy
d. astroturf

1.31 Examples:
a. capture
b. capable
c. captivate
d. captivity
e. capacious
f. capacity

1.32 Examples:
a. refer
b. confer
c. inference
d. reference

1.33 Examples:
a. recognize
b. pregnant
c. agnostic

1.34 Examples:
a. monograph
b. phonograph
c. autograph
d. geography
e. telegraph

1.35 Examples:
a. trajectory
b. interjection
c. objectivity
d. projection

1.36 Examples:
a. admonition
b. premonition
c. demonstrate
d. monitor

1.37 Examples:
a. mortify
b. mortician
c. post mortem
d. mortgage

1.38 Examples:
a. neurotic
b. neurosis
c. aneurysm
d. neuralgia

1.39 Examples:
a. pseudonym
b. synonym
c. homonym
d. antonym

1.40 Examples:
a. empathy
b. sympathy
c. psychopath
d. pathological

1.41 Examples:
a. disposition
b. deposit
c. imposition
d. imposter

1.42 Examples:
a. anarchist
b. monarch
c. architect
d. archangel

1.43 Examples:
a. epidermis
b. dermatitis
c. ectoderm
d. endoderm

1.44 Examples:
a. bigamy
b. monogamy
c. polygamy
d. gamete

1.45 Examples:
a. regeneration
b. generate
c. genus
d. genre

1.46 Examples:
   a. indigestion
   b. gestation
   c. gesture
   d. ingest

1.47 Examples;
   a. intermediary
   b. medium
   c. intermediate
   d. immediate

1.48 Examples:
   a. metrics
   b. meter
   c. metronome

1.49 Example: nascent

1.50 Examples:
   a. derogatory
   b. interrogative

1.51 Examples:
   a. compel
   b. repel
   c. expel
   d. impel
   e. dispel
   f. propel

1.52 Examples:
   a. explicate
   b. duplicate
   c. implicate

1.53 Examples:
   a. portable
   b. export
   c. reporter

1.54 Examples:
   a. expressive
   b. repress
   c. pressure

1.55 Examples:
   a. psychiatric
   b. psychological
   c. psychosomatic

1.56 Examples:
   a. static
   b. statute
   c. consistent
   d. style

1.57 Examples:
   a. scribble
   b. inscribe
   c. prescribe
   d. scribe

1.58 Any order:
   a. art
   b. craft
   c. skill

1.59 lingo or jargon

1.60 construction worker

1.61 fireman

1.62 a. potatoes (with cheese)
   b. meat, some vegetables (on a skewer)
   c. fish (in a greased paper bag)

1.63 a. maitre d'
   b. chef

1.64 c

1.65 a

1.66 c

1.67 b

1.68 Any order:
   a. igneous
   b. sedimentary
   c. metamorphic

1.69 meteorology

1.70 Any order:
   a. troposphere
   b. stratosphere
   c. ionosphere
   d. exosphere

1.71 a. shellfish
   b. spiders

1.72 personification

1.73 genre

1.74 protagonist

1.75 Either answer:
vocalists, music

1.76 master in the musical arts

1.77 elbow to longest finger - 18"

1.78 from thumb to little finger - 9"

1.79 12 x 12 or 144

1.80 Any order:
a. meter - length
b. kilogram - mass
c. second - time
d. degree celsius - temperature
e. ampere - electric current
f. candela - luminous intensity

1.81 g

1.82 d

1.83 a

1.84 c

1.85 e

1.86 f

1.87 b

1.88 TVA

1.89 scuba

1.90 RSVP

1.91 Zip

II. SECTION TWO

2.1 Topics will vary.

2.2 Subtopics will vary.

2.3 Paragraphs will vary.

2.4 disobedience is punished

2.5 faithful father

2.6 many reasons besides disobedience

2.7 negative to the Word of God

2.8 by bread alone

2.9 helper check

2.10 helper check

2.11 Outlines will vary.

2.12 Paragraphs will vary.

2.13 Only the first five sentences support the subject.

2.14 yes

2.15 no

2.16 This one was extremely disorganized. Hint: Using an outline should make a difference. The paragraph that follows an outline should be superior to those that are not written with an outline.

2.17 D - F

2.18 yes

2.19 one like the model in this section

2.20 yes

2.21 helper check

2.22 Father Firman invited his friend, Father Nulty, to come over and have dinner with him and Mrs. Stoner. The maid fixed a big dinner for the three of them and when they were ready for dessert, she brought a cake out for Father Nulty because it was his fifty-ninth birthday. The candles were lit and the lights were turned out so that he could blow out the candles in the dark. Mrs. Stoner then began to clear the table of the food and the dishes.

2.23 we, we, us, him, we, it, you, their, their, their, they, they, them, they

2.24 were taken, was made, was drunk, was eaten, were greeted, was thrown, was caught, were thrown, were whisked, was driven, were shed, were thrown, was had

2.25 cli - mat- ic

2.26 di - a - bol - i - cal

2.27 wor - ri - some

2.28 yes - ter - day

2.29 ful - fill - ment

2.30 ho - mo - ge - ne - ous

2.31 mar - riage - a - ble

2.32 pre - cip - i - tan - cy

2.33 el - i - gi - bil - i - ty

2.34 si - mul - ta - ne - ous

2.35 trans - con - ti - nen - tal

2.36 grat - i - fi - ca - tion

2.37 Mr. James Boone has lived at 328 Newton Terrace since April, 1963. He is a devoted outdoorsman even though he weighs only 130 pounds and stands a little over 5 feet. He walks five miles every day and treats his own illness, instead of send-ing for a doctor. Recently he per-suaded Honorable Smith (Hon. James Smith) and Reverend (or Rev.George) Bradley to accompany him to the V.A. Hospital, where the streets are quiet and the buildings are beautiful to the eye. Late in the afternoon he is likely to call his friends Charles Williams, George Glass, Elizabeth Bowen, and others [should omit and etc. Could use etc. alone, but not preferred and never use and with etc.] over for apples and popcorn before they go out for a long hike in the cool of the eve-

ning. Three hundred sixty-five days of the year, James is out there walking the highways and byways. He says if he had a dollar for every mile he's walked, he'd be a rich man

2.38 helper check

2.39 Hint:
List any of the preceding errors.

2.40 father

2.41 speech

2.42 poet

2.43 Mother

2.44 anniversary

2.45 Creek

2.46 German

2.47 physician

2.48 River

2.49 Rever Electric

2.50 ie

2.51 ei

2.52 ie

2.53 ei

2.54 ie; ei

2.55 ie; ei

2.56 ei

2.57 a. hungrier
b. tragedienne
c. tyrannical
d. fantasies
e. application
f. complies
g. funnier
h. busily
i. loneliness

j. likeliest
k. beautiful
l. monkeys
m. burial
n. enjoying
o. marriage
p. studying
q. luxurious
r. studious
s. denying
t. chimneys

2.58 a. propellant
     b. baggage
     c. foggy
     d. conference (exception to the rule)
     e. committee
     f. controlled
     g. reaped
     h. submitting
     i. hopped
     j. transmitting
     k. pocketing
     l. fitted
     m. preference (exception to the rule)
     n. commitment
     o. exceeding
     p. rebellious
     q. goddess
     r. thinner
     s. knitted
     t. dispelling

2.59 a. conceivable
     b. accommodation
     c. desirable
     d. advantageous
     e. nervous
     f. imaginary
     g. pursuable
     h. preceding
     i. merely
     j. suing
     k. useful
     l. changeable
     m. ninety
     n. forcibleness
     o. duly
     p. assemblage
     q. livable
     r. coming
     s. practical
     t. writing

2.60 a. drop the e
     b. consonant suffixes
     c. vowel suffixes

2.61 keep

2.62 drop

2.63 baby's; babies; babies'

2.64 fox's; foxes; foxes'

2.65 fireman's; firemen; firemen's

2.66 monkey's; monkeys; monkeys'

2.67 son-in-law's; sons-in-law; sons-in-law's

2.68 mouse's; mice; mice's

2.69 church's; churches; churches'

2.70 princess's; princesses; princesses'

2.71 sheep's; sheep; sheep's

2.72 child's; children; children's

2.73 Mr. Jones'; the Joneses; the Joneses

2.74 contralto's; contraltos; contraltos'

2.75 general's; generals; generals'

III. SECTION THREE

3.1 - 3.10 Hint:
     Be sure each sentence is complete.

3.1 S F

3.2 S F

3.3 S S

3.4 F S

3.5 S F

3.6 F S

3.7 F S

3.8 S F

3.9 F S

3.10 F F

3.11 We now know how hurricanes originate and how they affect ecology.

3.12 I am currently taking freshman English, a required course.

3.13 The ground was slippery, and I fell down.

3.14 To receive a certificate, six courses must be taken.

3.15 I shall meet you wherever you want me to.

3.16 Unless you have proof, don't make accusations.

3.17 Being a child of an army officer, Mary has lived all over the world.

3.18 Needing a loan, James applied at the financial aids office.

3.19 Having leaks in several places, the roof needed patching.

3.20 He never returned to the little mountain.

3.21 CS

3.22 F

3.23 F

3.24 S

3.25 CS

3.26 CS

3.27 F

3.28 S

3.29 F

3.30 S

3.31 - 3.40 Examples:

3.31 When one is discouraged, the Bible provides a blessed comfort.

3.32 Since I am naturally shy, dates became a burden to me.

3.33 Looking north, I can easily see our ranch.

3.34 While I was climbing up to the roof, the ladder slipped and made me fall.

3.35 When we ignored him, Johnny stopped having tantrums.

3.36 Since the chrysanthemums had been eaten by gophers, Dad set traps.

3.37 When Don was nine, his father died of a cerebral hemorrhage.

3.38 To sew properly, one should follow a pattern.

3.39 To achieve success in any field, one must persevere.

3.40 If you arrive at the fair early, you can see the winning entries.

3.41 The gardener is clean, eager, and hardworking.

3.42 Aunt Matilda loves to sew, cook, and ride horseback.

3.43 Writing compositions for English, learning a part in the play, and studying for a mathematics exam keeps me busy.

3.44 The President's goals are to improve education, to stabilize the economy, and to expand social programs

3.45 To watch educational television and to read good books are useful pursuits.

3.46 applicants; their

3.47 Neither; he prefers

3.48 dog; it

3.49 each; his

3.50 Neither; his

3.51 anyone; he

3.52 Anyone; he

3.53 person; him

3.54 YMCA; its

3.55 students; themselves

3.56 needs

3.57 is

3.58 stays

3.59 wins

3.60 has

3.61 after the light at the intersection of Gurley and Marina.

3.62 better than men do or better than they do men

3.63 Johnny never has studied geometry and he never will study it.

3.64 teachers

3.65 as law and medicine

3.66 admiration for and belief in

3.67 teacher check

3.68 a. Manner of expressing ideas in words.
b. Worn out by use
c. Words or phrases usually characterized by a special vividness of coloring and not generally used in formal English.
d. Used in everyday, informal talk, but not in formal English.
e. Stiffly dignified or formal.
f. Not definitely or precisely expressed

3.69 a. trite
b. vague
c. slang
d. stilted
e. vague
f. vague

1.1   Any order:
- a. Lord
- b. way
- c. statutes
- d. end
- e. understanding
- f. law
- g. heart

1.2   Any order:
- a. me
- b. thy
- c. I
- d. it
- e. me
- f. I
- g. thy
- h. I
- i. it
- j. my

1.3   personal

1.4   three

1.5   four

1.6   three

1.7   Any order:
- a. enemy
- b. bread
- c. water
- d. coals
- e. fire
- f. head
- g. Lord

1.8   Any order:
- a. thine
- b. him
- c. he
- d. him
- e. thou
- f. his
- g. thee

1.9   a. he
        b. thou

1.10   a. him
        b. him
        c. thee

1.11   a. thine
        b. his

1.12   Any ten; any order:
- a. one
- b. anyone
- c. someone
- d. no one
- e. none
- f. everyone
- g. anybody
- h. somebody
- i. nobody
- j. everybody

or anything, something, nothing, everything, much, either, neither, another, each (plural) many, all, others, few, several, some, most

1.13   a. relative
        b. interrogative

1.14   to reflect back on the antecedent or to intensify it.

1.15   a. direct object
        b. indirect object
        c. object of the preposition

1.16   The difference between a verb and a verb phrase is that a verb is one word; a verb phrase is more than one word.

1.17   future perfect tense

1.18   indicative mood, present tense, third person singular

1.19   present participle

1.20   subjunctive mood

1.21   a. froze
        b. freezing
        c. frozen

1.22   a. tore
        b. tearing
        c. torn

1.23   a. rode
      b. riding
      c. ridden

1.24   a. wrote
      b. writing
      c. written

       Any order:
1.25   a. am
      b. been
      c. do
      d. shall
      e. might
      f. is
      g. being
      h. does
      i. should
      j. must
      k. are
      l. have
      m. did
      n. will
      o. was
      p. has
      q. can
      r. would
      s. had
      t. could
      u. may
      v. be
      w. were

1.26   a. have eaten
      b. have eaten
      c. has eaten
      d. have eaten
      e. have eaten
      f. have eaten

1.27   a. sat
      b. laid

1.28   a. lay
      b. risen

1.29   a. lay
      b. lain

1.30   superficially

1.3.   sentimental

1.32   recklessly

1.33   reasonably

1.34   specially

1.35   a. more beautiful
      b. most beautiful

1.36   a. littler
      b. littlest

1.37   a. more
      b. most

1.38   a. more clearly; less clearly
      b. most clearly; least clearly

1.39   a. adjective
      b. adverb

1.40   a. adverb
      b. adjective

1.41-1.51 Examples:

1.41   I was hungry and (so) I ate.

1.42   I will go or I will stay.

1.43   I would go with you but (yet)
      I am not ready.

1.44   I am not sad yet (but) I am
      crying.

1.45   I could not play baseball yesterday
      (since) because I sprained my ankle.

1.46   Although it is raining this morn-
      ing, we plan to picnic this after-
      noon.

1.47   I will cook breakfast when (while,
      since, or because) you sleep late.

1.48   a. I rode in a taxi.
      b. noun

1.49   a. The taxi cab was yellow.
      b. adjective

1.50   a. The plane will taxi to the end
        of the runway.
      b. verb

1.51   a. Taxi!
       b. interjection

II.   SECTION TWO

2.1   Any order:
       a. S-V-O
       b. S-V
       c. S-V-IO-DO
       d. S-LV-N
       e. S-LV-Adj.
       f. inverted sentence
       g. question

2.2   teacher check

2.3   support (prove) a topic sentence

2.4   a. how
       b. what
       c. ask
       d. question

2.5   receiver of action (object)

2.6   direct object or receiver of action

2.7   a. receiver
       b. action

2.8   a. being
       b. past

2.9   subject-verb

2.10   (independent) main clauses or sentences

2.11   dependent (subordinate) clause

2.12   man
       brought
       (with him) (in the back row)
       friends DO

2.13   throw
       was
       (to first base)
       short SC

2.14   ocean
       stretched
       (before him) (to the horizon)

2.15   Diana
       gave
       (at the party)
       shoulder DO
       George IO

2.16   Esther
       showed
       (on Friday)
       necklace DO
       jeweler IO

2.17   father
       is
       citizen SC

2.18   you
       take
       (to your mother) (before morning)
       book DO

2.19   Needlepoint
       gives
       (of restfulness)
       her IO
       feeling DO

2.20   pickles
       taste
       (for me)
       sour SC

2.21   boundary
       is
       (of the Atlantic Ocean)
       edge SC

2.22   pilot
       told
       (about the damages) (to the wing)
       chief DO

2.23   minister
       called
       lady DO
       saint OC

2.24   Jason
       had
       (at his favorite Mexican restaurant)
       party DO

2.25 <u>car</u>
<u>is</u>
(for him) (of those new convertibles)
one SC

2.26 <u>committee</u>
<u>elected</u>
George DO
chairman OC

2.27 <u>Gerrards</u>
<u>consider</u>
son DO
genius OC

2.28 teacher check

III. SECTION THREE

3.1 than

3.2 under
or with, for, beside
3.3 as if (as though)

3.4 to

3.5 from

3.6 to

3.7 except

3.8 until

3.9 for

3.10 with

3.11 with

3.12 to

3.13 off

3.14 in

3.15 on

3.16 of

3.17 from

3.18 from

3.19 by

3.20 from

3.21 as

3.22 under

3.23 to

3.24 from

3.25 for
or to

3.26 connected with school-Anything

3.27 Hearing his name called-Joe

3.28 Roasted in aluminum foil-meats

3.29 crossing into Arizona-people

3.30 Cradled in her mother's arms-baby

3.31 injuring crops and destroying
property-Storms

3.32 covered-bridge

3.33 observing a crime-person

3.34 Seen by two women-accident

3.35 reading her Bible-girl

3.36 Hearing the siren-I

3.37 determined to get the truth-lawyer

3.38 Looking for evidence-inspector

3.39 Closed for the winter-boardwalk

3.40 Playing both football and baseball-
Nate

3.41 living, repairing cars
a. direct object
b. object of preposition

3.42 mimicking the other's voices, object
of preposition

3.43 Writing a research paper, subject

3.44 playing the piano, direct object

3.45 entertaining friends, predicate nominative (subject complement)

3.46 studying calculus, direct object

3.47 reducing taxes, object of preposition

3.48 Directing a play, subject

3.49 driving a hard bargain, object of preposition

3.50 Water-skiing, sailing, and swimming, subject

3.51 Cutting our own Christmas tree

3.52 Losing my wallet

3.53 By watching for sales

3.54 To help you, subject

3.55 to go with you to the store, direct object

3.56 to put my things, adjective

3.57 to study architecture, adverb

3.58 to assist you, direct object

3.59 to use the car tonight, adjective

3.60 to be restored as captain, subject complement

3.61 The weather bureau uses balloons to determine the temperature aloft.

3.62 It doesn't always save time to do something in a hurry.

3.63 The journalist took a job to get facts for an article.

3.64 Raspberry flavor is used in Kaopectate to mask the taste of the medicine

3.65 John had a black cat to prove he wasn't superstitious.

3.66 Although I wrote in time,

3.67 as soon as he comes in.

3.68 since she broke her leg.

3.69 provided that the owner repairs the roof.

3.70 in case I am called away.

3.71 After (When, As soon as)

3.72 Because (Since)

3.73 when (as, as soon as)

3.74 as (when)

3.75 that his dad gave him-knife

3.76 that so few people attended the party-shame

3.77 whose tickets have been punched-Those

3.78 who is a kind man-manager

3.79 whom I remember vaguely-man

3.80 which is near the ball park-Buddyburger

3.81 The poem Peg wrote for me was good enough to print.

3.82 He made some statements that had no foundation of fact.

3.83 Gerry won a swimming trophy of which he is very proud.

3.84 Mother, who saw the fire start, was sitting near the window.

3.85 Kim and Jane were discussing the play (that) they both had seen.

3.86 whatsoever He hath pleased direct object

3.87 that which concerneth me direct object

3.88   Whoso hearkeneth unto me
        subject

3.89   whom I will have mercy
        object of preposition

3.90   that they might be saved
        subject complement

3.91   that light is come into the world

3.92   his God

3.93   the chief of all their strength

3.94   his chosen

3.95   their Savior

3.96   Water being plentiful, the lawns
        were green all summer.

3.97   The hurricane season being over,
        people returned to the cottages
        on the beach.

1.1 less than 35
The time to complete each drill should gradually decrease.

1.2 less than 35

1.3 less than 35

1.4 less than 35

1.5 less than 35

1.6 20 seconds or less

1.7 20 seconds or less

1.8 less than 20 seconds

1.9 less than 20 seconds

1.10 less than 20 seconds

1.11 less than 20 seconds

1.12 less than 25 seconds
The key phrase appears seven times.

1.13 less than 25 seconds
The key phrase appears seven times.

1.14 less than 25 seconds
The key phrase appears six times.

1.15 less than 25 seconds
The key phrase appears six times.

1.16 less than 25 seconds
The key phrase appears seven times.

1.17 less than 25 seconds
The key phrase appears six times.

1.18 less than 25 seconds
The key phrase appears seven times.

1.19 less than 40 seconds

1.20 less than 40 seconds

1.21 less than 40 seconds

1.22 less than 40 seconds

1.23
a. no
b. yes
c. no
d. no
e. yes
f. no
g. no
h. no
i. yes
j. yes

1.24
a. yes
b. no
c. no
d. yes
e. no
f. no
g. yes
h. no
i. yes
j. yes

1.25
a. yes
b. no
c. yes
d. no
e. yes
f. yes
g. no
h. yes
i. yes
j. no

1.26
a. no
b. no
c. yes
d. yes
e. no
f. no
g. no
h. yes
i. no
j. no

1.27
a. Process analysis
b. One must be assertive (on the offensive) to win a game or live a life.

1.28
a. Cause/Effect
b. One is often vulnerable as a result of a victory.

1.29
a. Illustration/Example
b. Doctrine in the soul increases capacity for life, happiness, and blessing.

1.30 a. Contrast/Comparison
      b. Melchizedek differed greatly
         from the king of Sodom.

1.31 a. Classification/Division
      b. The Bible divides people into
         three groups: natural man,
         spiritual man, and carnal man.

1.32 a. Definition
      b. Job was a mature believer, posi-
         tive to God in everything.

1.33 a. 0
      b. F
      c. 0
      d. 0
      e. 0
      f. F
      g. F
      h. F
      i. 0
      j. F
      k. 0
      l. F
      m. F
      n. F
      o. 0

1.34 It is all fact.

1.35 four

1.36 no

1.37 The heading, Diet Tidbits.

1.38 None

1.39 yes

1.40 5, 6

1.41 2, 3, 4, 7, 9

1.42 8

1.43 both

1.44 Angels differ from men in important
      ways.

1.45 They don't have to eat to live.

1.46 not really
      Some food is called "angels' food,"
      implying that they eat.

1.47 Asaph and David

1.48 It sustained Elijah for 40 days and
      40 nights.

1.49 teacher check

1.50 yes

1.51 no

1.52 no

1.53 yes

1.54 no

1.55 no

1.56 implied

1.57 infer

1.58 implied

1.59 implied

1.60 infer

1.61 false

1.62 true

1.63 true

1.64 false

1.65 true

1.66 false

II. SECTION TWO

2.1 page 710

2.2 Books that Changed the World

2.3 page 31

2.4 page 4

2.5 29

2.6 **44**

2.7 53

2.8 Subjects are in capital letters, books are lower case.

2.9 28

2.10 550

2.11 Black Short Story Anthology

2.12 a. Jackson
b. Starrett

2.13 parentheses

2.14 aid to prepaid health plans

2.15 Sec. A page 8; the system cleaned up

2.16 120 - bed, "no-fulls" hospital

2.17 a. volunteer rent relief plan
b. **rent controls**
c. A
d. 25

2.18 a. B
b. 22

2.19 a. D
b. 21

2.20 a. Bobby Baker Tells All
b. Evita's Saga
c. World War I doves
d. Best Sellers
e. Outlaw's Ladies
f. N-8

2.21 N - 11 - 14

2.22 a. Dining Out
b. **N-6**

2.23 a. Hollywood Inverting in Broadway
b. Movie Notes
c. Here Come the Sequels
d. **N-9**

2.24 Page K-21

2.25 Henry Fuller (of Arizona)

2.26 rebuilding and renovation of Scoattadale's Hilton Inn

2.27 Page K-6

2.28 **600 - 625**

2.29 a. 5 p.m.
b. Thursday

2.30 271 - 9111

2.31 $3.00 plus tax

2.32 no

2.33 You check the ad and call in corrections the first day.

2.34 Between 7 a.m. and 9:30 a.m. Monday through Saturday and between 12 noon and 3 p.m. on Sunday.

2.35 that these are suffixes

2.36 Because it was dishonorable, humiliating, degrading

2.37 Ignominious = characterized by disgrace or shame.

2.38-2.41 (Refer to Websters' Seventh or Eighth New Collegiate Dictionary.)

2.38 **three**

2.39 **to heat up:** excite

2.40 Abbreviation / monogram for Jesus

2.41 Greek - transliterated to Late Latin

2.42 any of the five; all are quite common

2.43 Ill^2 is an adverb; ill^1 is an adjective

2.44 Ill^3 is a noun meaning trouble, misfortune, distress

2.45 One who holds a public, **civil, or** ecclestiastial office, a servant or minister of the king; a person appointed or elected to exercise some function in public life, take part in administration of municipal life. Early use - in the administration of law/justice.

2.46 a. Peace officer
      b. Police officer
      c. Sheriff's officer

2.47 August 23rd Sgt. McBryan was set upon by a crowd of roughs, who threw him down and kicked him brutally. In trying to use his revolver the officer shot himself through the left thumb.

2.48 1. One to whom a charge is committed, or who performs a duty, service, or function; a minister; an agent.
      2. One who holds an office, post or place.
      3. A petty officer of justice or of peace; a sheriff's sergeant, bailiff, catchpole, constable, jailer, executioner.
      4. A person holding a military or naval command, or occupying a position of authority in the army, navy, or mercantile marine; one holding a commission in army or navy.

2.49 cloak / hood

2.50 Malta

2.51 huke

2.52 cardigan or pullover knit with colorful bands of geometric design.

2.53 between the Orkneys and Shetlands

2.54 no

2.55 Is it a sash on a sash, shirt, halers, and hose?

2.56 Environmental aspects, Injurious effects

2.57 a. Prices
      b. Production methods
      c. Recovery methods
      d. Atlantic Ocean
      e. United States

2.58 U.S. News and World Report

2.59 June 28, 1999

2.60 Drug industry

2.61 a. Ready for a profit gusher, "Business Week"
      b. Why we'll never run out of oil, "Discover"

2.62 a. Dehumidifiers, seven
      b. Garden Tractors, twenty
      c. Exterior white house paint, 26
      d. Portable Window Fans, 29
      e. Sunglasses, 32

2.63 a. Metric Units
      b. Instrumentation
      c. Observation and Hypothesizing
      d. Scientific Notation
      e. Careers in Chemistry

2.64 a. Scientific Notation
      b. page 25

2.65 a. Length
      b. Volume
      c. Mass

2.66 a. Careers in Chemistry
      b. page 27 - 33

2.67 Preparation

2.68 a newcomer

2.69 New residents need to know who to call or where to go for services.

2.70 Trustworthiness; if he is well-known to be an honest workman

      Examples: To increase business; bring in new customers

2.71 teacher check

2.72 The telephone company

2.73 Because these ads are in competition with their yellow pages ads.

2.74 It probably costs less, people consult a directory, it's alphabetized.

2.75 These ads just give skeleton information, nothing outstanding.

2.76   555 - 3618

2.77   555 - 7300

2.78   771 - 9783

2.79   78 Arroyo Lane

2.80   136 Arroyo Lane

2.81   yes
        both are even numbers

2.82   one
        The Rev. after W. D. McNarie's
        name.

2.83   McMains Backhoe Service
        555-5055

2.84   Dr. Terrence Mc Naly
        555-5545

2.85   a. Indians of North America - The
           West - Wars
        b. The west - history
        c. Indians of North America - The
           West

2.86   seven

2.87   241

2.88   22 cm.

2.89   G.T 730.548 1977

2.90   Library of Congress

2.91   301.42

2.92   all three

2.93   Examples:
        De Vato, Bernard (ed.), The Journals
        of Lewis and Clark. (You could
        have looked under America—
        Discovery and exploration or U.S.
        History.)

2.94   a. John F. Kennedy
        b. Charles Dickens

2.95   a. A Connecticut Yankee in King
           Arthur's Court
        b. 813.4
           c625cb

III. SECTION THREE

3.1   Most lecture material will appear
        on tests. It may not be even
        mentioned in the textbook.

3.2   Take paper, pen, and book, sit
        near front, write main ideas, ask
        questions, organize (possibly type
        or rewrite) notes.

3.3   a. take notes on main points and
           key subpoints
        b. listen for teacher cues.
        c. abbreviate, use short cuts
        d. go over notes after class
        e. keep record of assignments,
           tests, papers, etc.

3.4   a. lecture
        b. textbook

3.5   doing research for a library or
        term paper

3.6   the use of an author's unique ideas
        or words without giving proper
        credit

3.7   word-for-word

3.8   A theory or an hypothesis setting
        forth the purpose of a paper which
        will be supported by specific facts
        or examples. A thesis states the
        purpose of a paper.

3.9   teacher check

3.10   friend check

3.11   helper check

1.1 the ability to use human language

1.2 He kept two babies isolated from human voices until they voluntarily made noises - the first noise was interpreted as Phrygian.

1.3 a sidedness of the brain. The left side of the brain controls the right side of the body.

1.4 the left side

1.5 use of language

1.6 nerve center for speech, visual and motor connectors

1.7 Example:
According to Peruvian Indian legend, he was a god who created the Incas and who taught them moral and social order, agriculture, and language.

1.8 Examples:
a. The gods created a man and a woman from two trees, an ash and an elm.
b. It was a gift to the man and the woman from the gods.

1.9 false

1.10 false

1.11 false

1.12 true

1.13 Any order:
a. Koiné Greek
b. Latin
c. Aramaic

1.14 the New Testament

1.15 c

1.16 b

1.17 e

1.18 g

1.19 d

1.20 h

II. SECTION TWO

2.1 Hint:
Study of grammar is practical preparation for college and the business world; knowledge of grammar makes effective communication possible. Use of language is a privilege, not a right - people have an obligation to God to use language well.

2.2 Examples:
a. names a person, place, or thing
b. used to make a statement, ask a question, or give a command
c. modifies a noun or noun substitute
d. modifies a word or word group other than a noun or pronoun
e. used to show the relation of a noun or noun substitute to the rest of the sentence
f. used to connect words, phrases, or clauses
g. used for simple exclamations Has no grammatical relationship to rest of sentence.
h. used as a noun substitute

2.3 noun

2.4 verb

2.5 noun

2.6 noun

2.7 adverb

2.8 adjective

2.9 a. a verb
     b. a noun
     c. Example:
         the relationship of the word
         rent to the other words in
         the sentence

2.10 Latin

2.11 a. three
      b. five

2.12 no

2.13 no

2.14 prescriptive

2.15 Any order:
      a. Charles Fries
      b. Edward Sapir
      c. Leonard Bloomfield

2.16 Any order:
      a. semantic fallacy
      b. logical fallacy
      c. normative fallacy

2.17 Any order:
      a. noun
      b. verb
      c. adjective
      d. adverb
      e. auxiliary
      f. preposition
      g. determiner
      h. conjunction
      i. pronoun
      j. interrogative
      k. intensive
      l. unnamed class

2.18 Either order:
      a. not
      b. there

2.19 empty words

2.20 intensifier

2.21 adverb

2.22 noun

2.23 verb

2.24 interrogative

2.25 empty words

2.26 preposition

2.27 auxiliary

2.28 Hint:
      Some class names are the same.
      Auxiliaries are classed as verbs
      in traditional grammar; determiners
      are classed as adjectives.
      Interrogatives overlap with
      pronouns and adverbs.

2.29 Example:
      The morphemic classification of a
      word depends primarily upon its
      form and the inflections, if any,
      that can be added to it. The
      syntactic classification of a
      word depends upon its use in a
      given sentence.

2.30 a. A sentence is composed of a
          noun phrase and a verb phrase.
      b. A noun phrase is composed of
          a determiner plus a noun.
      c. A substantive is composed of
          either an adjective or a noun
          phrase.
      d. A verb phrase is composed of
          a form of the verb *be* plus a
          substantive.

2.31 A kernel sentence is a sentence
      in its simplest form.

2.32 a. T
      b. KS
      c. T
      d. KS
      e. T

2.33   a.   <u>John;</u> <u>ate the cake</u>
       b.   Example:
          John qualifies as a noun
          phrase because it consists
          of a noun plus the determiner.
       c.   a kernel sentence

2.34   1957

2.35   multiplication

2.36   generate

2.37   competence

2.38   Example:
       He believed they went too deeply
       into structure, simply finding
       systems of elements without
       considering sentence structure.

2.39   a-this order; b-c either order:
       a.   phrase
       b.   transformational
       c.   morphophonemic

2.40   a.   negatives
       b.   passives
       c.   questions
       d.   deletions
       e.   rearrangement of elements

III.   SECTION THREE

3.1   Hint:
      Semantics is the study of word
      meanings.

3.2   a.   semantikos
      b.   signification

3.3   c

3.4   f

3.5   a

3.6   e

3.7   b

3.8   true

3.9   false

3.10   false

3.11   true

3.12   true

3.13   k

3.14   b

3.15   e

3.16   d

3.17   h

3.18   a

3.19   f

3.20   c

3.21   g

3.22   j

3.23   false

3.24   true

3.25   false

3.26   false

3.27   true

3.28   c

3.29   b

3.30   a

3.31   b

3.32   teacher check

3.33   c

3.34   f

3.35   a

3.36   d

3.37   b

3.38   teacher check

1.1 Stonehenge

1.2 Picts

1.3 a. tin mines
b. bronze

1.4 52

1.5 f

1.6 c

1.7 g

1.8 a

1.9 d

1.10 b

1.11 true

1.12 false

1.13 false

1.14 true

1.15 true

1.16 teacher check

1.17 c. and
he
again (ongan)
was
him
much (mycel)
many (menegu)
to
gather (gegaderod)
so (swa)
that (ðæt)
on
ship (scip)
land (lande)
hear (gehyrað)
out (ut)
seed (sæd)
sow (sawenne)
some (sum)

fell (fēoll)
lonely (weg)
come (comon)
over (ofer)
earth (eorðan)
up
thickness (þiccnesse)
sun (sunne)
shrank (forscranc)
thorns (þornas)
good (god)
land
brought (brōhte)
thirtyfold (þritigfealdne)
sixtyfold (syxtigfealdne)
hundredfold (hundfealdne)

1.18 Danish raids destroyed many manu-
scripts.

1.19 The language used in Anglo-Saxon
England. It is a descendent of
Germanic, a member of Indo-European.
It employs both inflection and
gender.

1.20 poet at court or a traveling poet.

1.21 based on half-line units consisting
of a phrase having two stresses.
A line of poetry was two half lines
separated by a pause, but joined
by alliteration.

1.22 a repetition of initial sounds in
two or more words.

1.23 a double metaphor, usually hyphenated

1.24 student check

1.25 comitatus

1.26 a good name that would outlive the
man.

1.27 Example:
an ideal character; almost superhuman

1.28 ship burials

1.29 Sutton Hoo

1.30   false

1.31   true

1.32   false

1.33   false

1.34   true

1.35   true

1.36   d

1.37   a

1.38   f

1.39   e

1.40   c

1.41   e

1.42   g

1.43   j

1.44   c

1.45   h

1.46   d

1.47   a

1.48   b

1.49   f

1.50   teacher check

1.51   a. patient
        b. not over-passionate
        c. not over-hasty of speech
        d. not over-weak or rash in war
        e. not over-glad
        f. not over-covetous
        g. never "over-eager" to boast

1.52   Example:
        That the riches of the world are
        waste. That all things pass and
        crumble.

1.53   teacher check

1.54   Either order:
        a. lone-flier
        b. whale-way

1.55   helper check

1.56   helper check

1.57   helper check

1.58   bookworm

1.59   fish and river

1.60   plough

1.61   anchor

1.62   oyster

1.63   false

1.64   true

1.65   true

1.66   false

1.67   false

II. SECTION TWO

2.1   d

2.2   h

2.3   c

2.4   a

2.5   e

2.6   i

2.7   b

2.8   g

2.9   false

2.10   true

2.11   true

2.12   true

2.13   false

2.14   true

2.15   true

2.16   failure

2.17   Any order:
a. trade and banking
b. cities
c. middle class

2.18   guilds

2.19   Any order:
a. shopkeepers
b. merchants
c. tradesmen

2.20   increased trade, cities, and middle class strength

2.21   Latin

2.22   a. French
b. Germanic language of Vikings

2.23   English or Anglo-Saxon

2.24   Either order:
a. Latin
b. French

2.25   b

2.26   d

2.27   a

2.28   f

2.29   c

2.30   an anonymous dramatic song passed through the oral tradition

2.31   simple story revealed through dialogue involving repetition and the use of many words. It uses the ballad stanza.

2.32   It consists of four lines of iambic pentameter, lines one and three have four accents, lines two and four have three accents. Lines two and four rhyme.

2.33   teacher check

2.34   Any order:
a. sermons
b. religious lyrics
c. debate

2.35   the transcience of life

2.36   feudal system

2.37   Any order:
a. honor
b. loyalty
c. bravery
d. courtesy

2.38   f

2.39   d

2.40   a

2.41   e

2.42   g

2.43   b

2.44   teacher check

III. SECTION THREE

3.1   d

3.2   b

3.3   a

3.4   b

3.5   helper check

3.6   Hint:
mention military service, service as diplomat, a customs official, in tne secret service, as a Justice of Peace, and member of Parliament, as Clerk of the kings, works and deputy forester.

3.7   teacher check

3.8   true

3.9   false

3.10   true

3.11   true

3.12 false

3.13 true

3.14 false

3.15 e

3.16 c

3.17 g

3.18 a

3.19 f

3.20 b

3.21 a. Dante's Divine Comedy
      b. Boccacio's Decameron
      c. Boccacio's Filostrata

3.22 Any order:
      a. Knight
      b. Squire
      c. Yeoman

3.23 Any order:
      a. Prioress
      b. Monk
      c. Friar
      d. Second Nun
      e. Nun's Priest

3.24 A pilgrimage to Canterbury.
      Pilgrims agree to tell tales
      along the way.

3.25 April (1. 1)

3.26 29 (1. 24)

3.27 Tabard (1. 20)

3.28 15 (1. 61)

3.29 a. Chivalry/military
      b. regular clergy
      c. middle class/bourgeoisie
      d. humble Christians
      e. rascals

3.30 To provide unity to the whole
      story, to add information and
      insight, to provide motivation
      for the tales to reveal Chaucer's
      attitudes.

3.31 teacher check

3.32 teacher check

3.33 The widow lives in a very modest
      cottage: her roaster is regally
      fine in appearance. Very ordinary
      happenings are described in ele-
      vated terms.

3.34 He gave in to flattery.

3.35 Chaunticleer tricks the fox into
      speaking.so that the rooster escapes.

3.36 d

3.37 f

3.38 a

3.39 e

3.40 c

3.41 teacher check

1.1 "Song" from Cymbeline or "Triumph of Charis"

1.2 "Golden Slumbers Kiss Your Eyes"

1.3 "Song" from Cymbeline

1.4 "The Song" from Much Ado About Nothing

1.5 "The Man of Life Upright"

1.6 Charis beauty and charm triumph over all men (all hearts do duty to her beauty and all wish to be by her side)

1.7 "the daisies kiss our feet" The poet is showing the new, young (only as high as our feet) daisies bending and growing in springtime.

1.8 a. frisk, play
    b. kiss
    c. "The fields breathe sweet"
    d. sense of hearing

1.9 f

1.10 e

1.11 d

1.12 a

1.13 c

1.14 a. garden
     b. roses and lilies
     c. pearl
     d. rosebuds filled with snow
     e. angels
     f. bended bow

1.15 The women's lips are compared to cherries that none may buy (kiss) until she (like a street vendor) cries "Cherry-Ripe."

1.16 thirty feet (5 x 6 = 30)

1.17 His bones have become coral; his eyes have become pearls.

1.18 Anything of him that "doth fade cannot escape a sea-change. Therefore, all of his body can be changed. Only the spirit, or soul, does not fade and, therefore, will not suffer a "sea-change."

1.19 This song could offer some consolation. It does not stress the decay of the body but rather a transformation into something "rich and strange."

1.20 The first line: "Full fathom five thy father lies"

1.21 The "f" cannot be repeated quickly. The slowness of the repetition creates a somber, serious tone and gives a feeling of the depth of the ocean.

1.22 personification (of the moon) and alliteration (repetition of "s").

1.23 The fourth line alludes to Cupid

1.24 c

1.25 f

1.26 a

1.27 b

1.28 e

1.29 g

1.30 abba/abba/cd/cd/ee

1.31 abba/abba/cd/cd/ee

1.32 Sonnet XXXI best illustrates the division. In the octave the poet observes that the moon is in love. In the sestet he gives his reaction to the fickleness of woman's love.

1.33 Lines 5 and 6: My love contains in herself all the riches of the world.

1.34 a. his lady's eyes
      b. his lady's lips
      c. his lady's teeth
      d. his lady's forehead
      e. his lady's locks of hair
      f. his lady's hands

1.35 Her fairest treasure is her mind
      (which is adorned with many
      virtues).

1.36 false

1.37 true

1.38 false

1.39 true

1.40 true

1.41 true

1.42 false

1.43 false

1.44 true

1.45 true

1.46 sun

1.47 personification of the sun (it is
      given a complexion)

1.48 the summer is less lovely and less
      temperate; it has rough winds and
      is sometimes too hot; it does not
      last (too short a lease)

1.49 things change by chance or by
      natures course (time)(line 8)

1.50 this poem

1.51 the poet immortalizes the subject
      in the poem that will live as long
      as persons can breathe and see
      (until the end of time)

1.52 abab/cdcd/efef/gg

1.53 abab/cdcd/efef/gg

1.54 anything that hinders or obstructs
      or prevents

1.55 True love remains constant in all
      difficulties and situations.

1.56 Love is compared to a star that
      remains fixed and constant to
      guide ships.

1.57 The personification often occurs
      at New Years. At this time Old
      Father Time leaves and "baby New
      Year" enters.

1.58 a. If rest and sleep (which are
          only imitations of death) are
          pleasurable then death must
          be even more so.
      b. Death is a slave to fate,
          chance, kings, and desperate
          men--all of these can cause
          death.
      c. Death dwells with unpopular
          elements (poison, war, sick-
          ness.)
      d. Drugs can "deaden" as well as
          death.
      e. Above all death is not really
          a killer but is instead a
          giver of life.

1.59 The Christian belief is life after
      death: after death, "we wake
      eternally."

1.60 abba/abba/cddc/ee

1.61 Example:
      The King James Version states:
      "Translated out of the original
      tongues and with the former trans-
      lations diligently compared and
      revised by His Majesty's special
      command.

1.62 a. 150
      b. nineteenth

1.63 a. kings, princes, judges, young
          men and maidens, old men and
          children

      b. stormy wind
      c. dragons, beasts, cattle,
          creeping things, flying fowl
      d. sun, moon, stars, heavens

1.64　a.　old and greyheaded

　　　b.　a metaphor compares God to a rock and a fortress

1.65　a metaphor compares "we" to "sheep"

1.66　a.　snow (verse 7)

　　　b.　tongue, lips, mouth (verses 14 and 15)

　　　c.　"A broken and contrite heart" (repentance)

1.67　a.　Psalm 148

　　　b.　Psalm 100

　　　c.　Psalm 71

　　　d.　Psalm 51

1.68　Example:
The Good Samaritan and The Mustard Seed. Look up "parable" in a dictionary or concordance of the King James Version for a complete list of parables.

1.69　As a father forgives and rejoices when his son repents, so too does God forgive His children when they repent.

1.70　The Pharisees criticized Jesus for associating with sinners. Jesus told the story to illustrate that God cares for sinners and is eager for their repentance.

1.71　a.　Paul explains the qualities and absolute importance of charity.

　　　b.　Words, without charity as a motive, are meaningless.

　　　c.　sense of hearing

　　　d.　Example: In this life we do not see (understand) all, so we must live by faith.

1.72　a

1.73　b

1.74　b

1.75　teacher check

II. SECTION TWO

2.1　Latin

2.2　cycle

2.3　a.　at a fixed station

　　　b.　on pageant wagons

2.4　Examples; Any order:

　　　a.　originally an individual scene in a medieval mystery play or any of the wagons on which mystery plugs were performed

　　　b.　a spectacular exhibition, elaborate parade, etc., as a procession with floats

　　　c.　an outdoor drama, celebrating an historical event or presenting, with local actors, the history of a community, or empty pomp or display; mere show

2.5　c

2.6　a

2.7　b

2.8　a

2.9　b

2.10　c

2.11　d

2.12　b

2.13　e

2.14　c

2.15　f

2.16　The Globe was built in 1599.

2.17　The Globe burned down during a performance of Henry VIII.

2.18　The rebuilt Globe (rebuilt in 1614) was pulled down to make room for housing.

2.19   false

2.20   false

2.21   true

2.22   false

2.23   true

2.24   false

2.25   Either order:
a. The Elizabethan adopted and adapted physical elements and the inyards: the jutting stage, the uncovered area in front of the stage the covered balconies.
b. Elizabethan drama developed the one-dimensional characters and conflicts of the morality plays into three dimensional ones.

2.26   Example:
a maker or creator of plays

2.27   a poet

2.28   a. 1564
b. 1585
c. 1616

2.29   Example:
Comedy is defined as "something funny."

2.30   Example:
Tragedy is defined as "something sad."

2.31   England was enjoying success: she ruled the seas, enjoyed religious peace at home, and led in the race for an empire. The defeat of the Spanish Armada especially boosted national pride.

2.32   Shakespeare wrote many poems and dramas.

2.33   In thirty years or less (Shakespeare probably did not write before he went to London in 1585),

Shakespeare produced thirty-eight plays, two long narrative poems, 154 sonnets, and several other poems.

2.34   New words were borrowed from Greek and Latin because the Renaissance Elizabethan's read and admired the Greek and Latin classics. This familiarity encouraged them to borrow words.

2.35   The written word provided a consistency in spelling, grammar, and vocabulary.

2.36   Any order:
a. [Obs] to call or address (a person
b. [Archaic] to call by name
c. The word is not in use today

2.37   Rash still means quick but implies recklessness.

2.38   teacher check

2.39   b

2.40   a

2.41   b

2.42   b

2.43   a. false
b. false
c. true
d. false
e. true

2.44   a. 3
b. 1
c. 6
d. 4
e. 2
f. 5

2.45   It "started" [jumped] "like a guilty thing" and disappeared.

2.46   The action might indicate the Ghost is evil.

2.47   They have seen the Ghost twice by the end of the scene.

2.48 The Ghost was dressed in full armor.

2.49 The old King Hamlet had killed in battle the king of Norway and won some of his lands. Now the Norwegian king's nephew was preparing to avenge his uncle's death and win back the land.

2.50 He is swift to act and determined in his resolutions.

2.51 Horatio was a scholar (a student).

2.52 a. true   2.53 a. 5
     b. true   b. 1
     c. false   c. 3
     d. false   d. 4
     e. true   e. 2
     f. true

2.54 Any order:
     a. His father's death distresses him.
     b. He is upset that Claudius, whom Hamlet considers inferior, has taken his father's throne and wife.
     c. His mother's hasty marriage to Claudius leads Hamlet to believe that she did not really love King Hamlet and that she is untrustworthy.

2.55 Hamlet puns on the words "sun" and "son." He has expresses resentment at the fact that he is now Claudius's stepson.

2.56 a. false
     b. true
     c. true

2.57 a. 1
     b. 4
     c. 2
     d. 3

2.58 Laertes believes that because of Hamlet's noble birth he is not free to do (or marry) as he pleases. Hamlet's actions must be based on a consideration of his position in life.

2.59 "To thine own self be true. . . [then] you canst not . . . be false to any man."

2.60 a. true
     b. false
     c. true
     d. false
     e. true

2.61 a. 6
     b. 1
     c. 3
     d. 7
     e. 5
     f. 8
     g. 4
     h. 2

2.62 King Hamlet was in the orchard.

2.63 King Hamlet was sleeping when he was killed.

2.64 Claudius poured poison in King Hamlet's ear.

2.65 Yes. Hamlet talks so strangely that Horatio says he uses "wild and whirling words."

2.66 Hamlet is not happy. He says, "O cursed spite that ever I was born to set it right."

2.67 affectionate, or loving, tender

2.68 twelve (including the Ghost speaking in Scene 5)

2.69 The relationship is not good. Denmark is preparing its military to ward off a possible attack by Norway.

2.70 a. false
     b. false
     c. true

2.71 a. 2
     b. 4
     c. 3
     d. 1

2.72 Example:
     The technique is not an acceptab Christian method of searching for truth.

2.73 Hamlet has already indicated in Act I that he may sometimes pretend to be mad. Another possible reason is that his disillusionment with his mother has motivated him to test another woman, Ophelia.

2.74 a. false
b. false
c. true

2.75 a. 1
b. 5
c. 2
d. 6
e. 3
f. 7
g. 4

2.76 a. the death of his father
b. the death of his father plus his mother's hasty remarriage
c. Ophelia's rejection of his love
d. disappointment because he was not named king after his father's death

2.77 The king of Norway ordered Fortinbras to stop plotting against Denmark and to direct his attention to the Poles.

2.78 "Now I am alone" introduces the soliloquy "O, what a rogue and peasant slave am I!"

2.79 The Ghost may have been an evil spirit, or devil, so Hamlet could not act without being sure that Claudius is guilty.

2.80 Because Hamlet is not sure of the true nature of the Ghost, he must make sure that the King is guilty. He, therefore, will use the play to be performed that night as a test of Claudius's guilt and will take action accordingly.

2.81 The major conflict is the one between Hamlet and Claudius. Other conflicts have been started in Act II: conflict between Hamlet and himself; conflict between Hamlet and Gertrude; conflict between Hamlet and Ophelia; conflict between Norway and Denmark.

2.82 a. false
b. true
c. false
d. true
e. true
f. true

2.83 a. 4
b. 1
c. 3
d. 2

2.84 His excuse then was that he had not yet been sure if the Ghost was an evil or good spirit.

2.85 a. "Let the doors be shut upon him [Polonius], that he may play the fool nowhere but in his own house."
b. "Those that are married already—all but one--shall live; the rest shall keep as they are."

2.86 a. false
b. true
c. false

2.87 a. 2
b. 5
c. 3
d. 1
e. 4

2.88 The play is a trap to catch Claudius if he is guilty. Later, when Hamlet thinks he is stabbing Claudius he says, "How now--I a rat?"

2.89 Hamlet is extremely excited, almost hysterical with happiness because he has proved Claudius guilty.

2.90 Hamlet, now convinced of Polonius's guilt, is eager for revenge and determined to take action. He declares, "I could drink hot blood."

2.91 a. true
b. false
c. false

2.92 a. 3
     b. 1
     c. 4
     d. 2

2.93 Hamlet reasons that if he kills
Claudius while he is at prayer,
Claudius will go to heaven and
therefore Hamlet would be doing
him a favor. Hamlet decides to
wait and kill him when he is in
sin, just as Claudius killed King
Hamlet without giving him a chance
to repent.

2.94 He will not give up the things
for which he murdered: the throne,
the queen, ambition, and power.

2.95 Example:
Claudius means that prayers are
not prayers unless a person means
the words and sincerely intends
to do good.

2.96 a. false
     b. false
     c. true
     d. false
     e. true
     f. true

2.97 a. 2
     b. 4
     c. 3
     d. 1
     e. 5
     f. 6

2.98 made in imitation of something
genuine with intention to deceive
or defraud

2.99 a. She flees him because she
does not know if he is mad
or sane.
     b. She is even more afraid after
he kills Polonius.
     c. Finally she is frightened
because he speaks to a ghost
she cannot see.

2.100 When Hamlet implies that his
mother helped murder his father,
she responds in surprise, "As
kill a king?"

2.101 Saying that he trusts them as
much as he would snakes ("adders
fanged"), he will protect himself
and will try to outsmart them and
turn whatever trick may be
involved to work on them.

2.102 Polonius's death caused Hamlet
to "pack him up" (carry him out
of the room) and will probably
cause Hamlet to "pack his bags"
(leave the country).

2.103 a. false
     b. false
     c. false
     d. false

2.104 a. 3
     b. 5
     c. 1
     d. 2
     e. 4

2.105 Hamlet has seen that both Norway
and Poland are willing to lose
lives and money over an insigni-
ficant piece of land (an "eggshell,
Hamlet says). Hamlet then reflects)
that he has a much greater cause
to take courageous action.

2.106 a. true
     b. true
     c. false
     d. true

2.107 a. 3
     b. 1
     c. 4
     d. 2

2.108 After Laertes learns of the death
of his father, he immediately
makes a resolution to act and get
revenge. He is quicker to decide
and act than Hamlet.

2.109 a. true
     b. true
     c. true
     d. false
     e. true

2.110 a. 2
       b. 4
       c. 1
       d. 3

2.111 a. He does not want to hurt
           Gertrude, who loves Hamlet.
       b. He is afraid the Danish people
           might not believe the kings
           accusations against Hamlet,
           whom they like.

2.112 a. Laertes will dip the tip of
           his sword in poison.
       b. Claudius will offer Hamlet
           a cup of poisoned wine.

2.113 a. false
       b. true
       c. true
       d. true

2.114 a. 2
       b. 3
       c. 5
       d. 1
       e. 4

2.115 The rich and the noble get
       privileges and exceptions that
       are denied to the poor.

2.116 a gravemaker: the houses he
       builds last till doomsday

2.117 No one can escape death. The
       strong and the weak, the rich
       and the poor--all must die.

2.118 Hamlet believes that Laertes'
       grief is showy and exaggerated
       and insists that his own love
       for Ophelia was greater and
       more sincere than Laertes'.

2.119 a. false
       b. false
       c. true
       d. true
       e. false
       f. true
       g. true

2.120 a. 6
       b. 1
       c. 9
       d. 10
       e. 2

       f. 11
       g. 4
       h. 14
       i. 5
       j. 7
       k. 8
       l. 3
       m. 12
       n. 13
       o. 15

2.121 Hamlet and Laertes almost
       accomplished a truce, a recon-
       ciliation that could have
       cancelled the fencing match.

2.122 Four people die at the court--
       Gertrude, Claudius, Laertes, and
       Hamlet. Two people die in
       England--Rosencrantz and Guilden-
       stern.

2.123 a. exciting force
       b. Hamlet sees the Ghost for
           the first time.

2.124 a. tragic force
       b. Hamlet's stabbing of Polonius

2.125 based on what is called "Freytag's
       pyramid."

       1. exposition
       2. rising action
       3. climax
       4. falling action
       5. catastrophe

       Number 4 on the chart could be as
       long as number 2; however, falling
       action, is usually shorter than
       rising action. This chart is
       based on what is called "Freytag's
       pyramid."

2.126 The main conflict is the one
       between Hamlet and Claudius.

2.127 Hamlet is torn between his
       emotional desire to take revenge
       and his natural tendency to think
       and reflect rather than act.

2.128 In a sense, Hamlet's conflict is resolved by forces outside himself. He was forced to kill Rosencrantz and Guildenstern to save his own life. He is also basically forced into a duel (even though logic and Horatio told him he would lose) in which he kills Claudius and he himself dies. Claudius's death, however, was not the result of a deliberate plan of action.

2.129 One of the forces over which a person has no control is the workings of a divinity.

2.130 "Are not two sparrows sold for a farthing? and one of them shall not fall on the ground without your Father."

2.131 helper check

2.132 Hamlet's flaw is his inability to make a decision and then take action to carry it out.

2.133 a. The tragic hero is usually of noble birth; his death affects a large number of people.
b. Comic relief is used to ease the tension of the tragedy.
c. Suspense is built by both internal and external conflicts.
d. The hero is destroyed by his tragic flaw.
e. Supernatural elements (Ghost) are present.

2.134 Examples:
a. Hamlet is an intelligent young man with high ideals whose tendency is to think deeply rather than act quickly.
b. Although she was hasty and foolish in marrying Claudius, Gertrude is well-intentioned (though weak) and truly loves Hamlet.
c. Claudius is a practical politician ("explains" his actions to his courtiers so they won't be upset); he is hungry for material power and prestige.

d. Polonius is practical and experienced in the ways of the world (appearances are important); he is a busybody
e. Ophelia is simple, polite, and obedient.
f. Laertes is quick to decide and quick to act.
g. Horatio represents an ideal balance between reason and emotion.

III. SECTION THREE

3.1 Examples:
1. Keep your thoughts to yourself; don't reveal everything you are thinking.
2. Act only on moderate thoughts.
3. Be friendly, but not too friendly.
4. Cling tightly to tried-and-true friends.
5. Do not waste time on acquaintances that will never be true friends.
6. Try to avoid quarrels but once you are in one, fight to win.
7. Listen to everyone; speak (reveal yourself) to only a few.
8. Listen to other's opinions but keep yours to yourself.
9. Buy good quality, but not gaudy, clothes (because "Clothes make the man").
10. Do not borrow or lend - in loaning, you may never again see the item loaned or the friend to whom you loaned it; in borrowing, you dull your friendship.
11. Be true to yourself and you will not (cannot) be false to anyone.

3.2 Be true to yourself.

3.3 Examples; Any order:
a. the art of making judgments
b. a review or article expressing such analysis
c. finding fault
d. the art principles or methods of a critic or critics

3.4   to hold a mirror up to nature;
      that is, to show life as it is
      without artificiality

3.5   The following ideas can be
      supported by the text of Act I.
      1. He was a strong and victorious
          king (defeated Norway and
          Poland).
      2. He was valiant.
      3. He was esteemed by the Danes
          and by "this side of our
          known world."
      Any other conclusion is acceptable
      only if it is supported by
      evidence from the text.

3.6   a. Hamlet procrastinates. He
          delays his action to take
          revenge and rationalizes
          his reasons for doing so.
      b. Laertes demands explanation
          and immediately decides to
          avenge his father's death
          and is willing to carry out
          his decision in a fencing
          match with a poisoned sword.
      c. Fortinbras takes immediate
          action to avenge his father's
          death and raises an unlawful
          army to attack Denmark.

3.7   He definitely establishes his
      guilt and responsibility for his
      father's death. He is troubled
      by the guilt but will not take
      the steps (give up throne, queen
      and power) to rid himself of his
      guilt.

3.8   He is a man more concerned about
      making a good impression than
      leading a good life based on
      principles.

3.9   By "right," Hamlet should have
      been king after his father's
      death. By "right" of medieval
      standards, Hamlet could (should)
      avenge his father's death.

3.10 Christian standards and the modern
      system of trial by jury forbid
      Hamlet's seeking of revenge.

3.11 eight: Ophelia, Gertrude,
      Claudius, Laertes, Polonius,
      Hamlet, Rosencrantz, and Guilden-
      stern.

3.12 Revenge brings violence and
      destruction; it upsets the
      natural order and balance of
      existence.

3.13 Example:
      The message is valuable; revenge
      can create a godless chaos.

3.14 Any order:
      a. dialogues
      b. soliloquies
      c. asides

3.15 What does the writer say?

3.16 What is the worth of the writing
      saying it?

3.17 How does he say it?

3.18 teacher check

3.19 teacher check

3.20 teacher check

3.21 teacher check

3.22 false

3.23 false

3.24 true

3.25 false

1.1 The Commonwealth was the Puritan government after Charles I's execution, lasting until the Restoration in 1660.

1.2 The Parliamentary forces (or Puritans, Roundheads) fought against the King's forces (or Royalists, Cavaliers)

1.3 No, because they did not like their tax money supporting a church they did not agree with, or a corrupt king controlling the church.

1.4 Charles I recessed Parliament from 1629 to 1640 and preferred Catholic ritual. Laws were forcing conformity to the Church of England.

1.5 Charles II was invited back to England as King.

1.6 b

1.7 d

1.8 a

1.9 **followers of James II, who was driven from England in 1688**

1.10 William and Mary were invited to take the throne, causing Parliament to control the succession to the throne.

1.11 true

1.12 false

1.13 false

1.14 true

1.15 true

1.16 false

1.17 true

1.18 false

1.19 false

1.20 true

1.21 critical responsibility, use of reason and logic, use of realism, and suspicion of shows of emotional, religious views

1.22 moral themes, sentimental tone, lyrical movement, emotional appeal, emphasis on common man or the past, interest in the supernatural, and interest in melancholy

1.23 a fictitious narrative with a closely knit plot, of epic scope, and a unity of theme

II. SECTION TWO

2.1 c

2.2 a

2.3 b

2.4 b

2.5 a

2.6 b

2.7 d

2.8 c

2.9 a

2.10 c

2.11 a

2.12 b

2.13 d

2.14 b

2.15 c

2.16   d

2.17   d

2.18   Milton asks how he can use his poetic talent when he is blind.

2.19   Milton assures himself that he must accept what God has given him, that he must "stand and wait."

2.20   true

2.21   false

2.22   true

2.23   true

2.24   true

2.25   true

2.26   false

2.27   **when the angel Michael convinces him that Christ will save mankind**

2.28   **He prevents God from destroying mankind.**

2.29   d

2.30   d

2.31   a

2.32   c

2.33   c

2.34   yes

2.35   **no**
His hate and revenge will be unchanged (lines 252-55).

2.36   **Hell is so dark that even its flames produce no light (light is usually symbolic of God's truth).**

2.37   a

2.38   c

2.39   d

2.40   c

2.41   b

2.42   S's sound like a fire hissing.

2.43   He uses active verbs to show birds in flight.

2.44   c

2.45   b

2.46   d

2.47   Whereas Satan has made a hell within himself, Adam will possess a paradise within himself by living a life full of faith, virtue, patience, temperance, and love.

2.48   Jesus' redemption of man

2.49   The word <u>as</u> is a clue that a stated comparison follows. It means that the angels come down from the hill lightly, like an evening mist glides over a marsh.

2.50   teacher check

2.51   false

2.52   false

2.53   true

2.54   false

2.55   true

2.56   false

2.57   b

2.58   d

2.59   c

2.60   false

2.61   true

2.62 a

2.63 c

2.64 a

2.65 d

2.66 Hint:
the physical appearance of the man (dressed in rags, held a book, burden on his back); the actual hearing of what the characters said

2.67 b

2.68 b

2.69 c

2.70 d

2.71 b

III. SECTION THREE

3.1 false

3.2 true

3.3 true

3.4 true

3.5 c

3.6 c

3.7 b

3.8 d

3.9 a

3.10 b

3.11 d

3.12 c

3.13 a

3.14 d

3.15 **Times and lengths of time are given**

("half an hour," "about eight o'clock in the evening," "above nine hours") to give a diary effect. Descriptions of the water and grass are given. Gulliver's reactions and feelings are given.

3.16 probably the type of person who would do anything to gain political power

3.17 the "guilt by association" method: the comparison of the satirized object to something undignified

3.18 yes, the king shows much common sense

3.19 He compares humans to insects.

3.20 Gulliver talks of trade, wars, political and religious disagreements, all problems of Swift's England.

3.21 No, they do not have the "perfections" or moral abilities required for their jobs.

3.22 Gulliver sees an island floating in the air

3.23 This country could symbolize a people whose studies and ideas are so abstract that they cannot be footed on "solid ground," on common sense.

3.24 A flapper is necessary because their minds are usually so absorbed in abstract thought that they are unable to carry on their **daily lives without the attention-getting instruments.**

3.25 b

3.26 d

3.27 d

3.28 teacher check

IV. SECTION FOUR

4.1 c

4.2   b

4.3   c

4.4   a

4.5   Possible answers:
       The Gentleman's Magazine, The Rambler,
       The Universal Chronicle

4.6   A Dictionary of the English Language, The
       Lives of the English Poets, Rasselas

4.7   false

4.8   false

4.9   true

4.10   true

4.11   true

4.12   true

4.13   c

4.14   a

4.15   d

4.16   c

4.17   a

4.18   b

4.19   a

4.20   b

4.21   b

4.22   As a rabbit returns to a safe place after being
       chased, the poet had also hoped to return to
       the quiet village.

4.23   singing milk-maid, lowing cows, gabbing
       geese, children's play, dog's bark, laughter,
       nightingale call

4.24   c

4.25   a

4.26   b

4.27   c

4.28   a

4.29   teacher check

1.1   a.   the land of Moriah
       b.   **very little; a thicket is**
          mentioned

1.2   a.   Abraham and Isaac
       b.   Example:
          Abraham loves Isaac, his only
          son, who is only a boy small
          enough to be lifted. Abraham
          is a God-fearing man.

1.3   a.   6
       b.   3
       c.   1
       d.   7
       e.   2
       f.   5
       g.   4

1.4   no

1.5   Example:
Abraham is blessed by God for
his obedience and faith.

1.6   Example:
Devotion to God must take
precedence over all earthly
things, even the love for an
only child.

1.7   a.   sixteen
       b.   because her brother is seven-
          teen and she is a year
          younger

1.8   a.   a friend of Kelly's
       b.   Example:
          She is used to reveal Kelly's
          character. The one-sided con-
          versation shows Kelly's unwil-
          lingness to cheat or to displease
          her parents.

1.9   Evelyn is found; Robbie admits
that he is wrong; Kelly thinks
of a poem.

1.10 a.   Kelly is assigned a poem but
          finds it impossible to write.
      b.   Kelly's parents leave for
          the weekend, putting Robbie
          in charge.
      c.   Evelyn interrupts Kelly's

futile attempt to write.
      d.   Kelly hurts Evelyn's feelings
      e.   Kelly asks Robbie to help her
          write a poem.
      f.   Robbie refuses to help.
      g.   Kelly declines an opportunity
          to cheat on the assignment.
      h.   Robbie discovers that Evelyn
          has run away.
      i.   Kelly looks for Evelyn.
      j.   Robbie catches up with Kelly.
      k.   Kelly and Robbie find Evelyn.
      l.   Kelly thinks of a poem.

1.11 a.   when Evelyn runs away (or, when
          Kelly reads the note)
      b.   when Evelyn is found
      c.   when friendly relationships
          are restored and Kelly thinks
          of a poem

1.12 Example:
Kelly's attitude would have been
significantly different. The conflict between her and her sister
might have been avoided.

1.13 the effect upon Kelly

1.14 the radio, the telephone, the terms
<u>family room</u> and <u>easy chair</u>.

1.15 the bare elm trees, the cloudy sky,
the coats, the mud

1.16 The ordinary furnishings contribute
a feeling of casual intimacy. When
the story moves outdoors into the
cold winter weather, the tension
is increased.

1.17 Example:
a sense of her own intellectual
superiority, a tendency to be
irritable or brusque

1.18 Example:
sense of responsibility, faith in
God, love of family

1.19 a.   0
       b.   ✓

c. ✓
d. 0
e. ✓
f. ✓
g. ✓

1.20 Example:
Because Robbie is quite intelligent and is apparently accus-
tomed to succeeding in everything
with little effort, he does not
understand the agony his sister
feels over her failure to complete an assignment. Because
he cannot empathize with her,
he cheerfully dismisses her
problem as unimportant. In
addition he expects her, as an
honor student and as his sister,
to be able to match his performance. He is thoughtless and
not particularly observant, but
he is not deliberately uncharit-
able.

1.21 Hint:
Use a complete sentence different
from that in the content. Be
certain that you can justify
your statement by using evidence
from the story.

1.22 a. capable of being touched or
felt
b. spherical; round

1.23 a window with sashes (frames)
that open at the sides

1.24 because it has been leaned upon
by many elbows

1.25 a. Example:
A poem should seem to be an
experience rather than something read and it should move
the heart as the flight of
birds does, wordlessly
Example:
Old medallions, though
silent, hold many memories
for the old soldiers who
often hold them.

1.26 the art of poetics

1.27 Poetry is an emotional, not an
intellectual, experience.

1.28 a. They have ears, but they hear
not; noses have they, but they
smell not.
b. two paradoxes

1.29 a. As for man, his days are as
grass: as a flower of the
field, so he flourisheth.
b. two similes

1.30 a. He shall cover thee with his
feathers, and under his wings
shalt thou trust; his truth
shall be thy shield and
buckler.
b. implied metaphor, metaphor

1.31 a. Their poison is like the poison
of a serpent: they are like
the deaf adder that stoppeth
her ear.
b. implied metaphor, two similes

1.32 a. Nor for the pestilence that
walketh in darkness; nor for
the destruction that wasteth
at noonday
b. personification (two examples)

1.33 a. anapestic tetrameter
b. iambic pentameter
c. trochaic tetrameter

1.34 alliteration (repetition of "f"
sound)

1.35 shout, about (Line 15)

1.36 shout

1.37 a. T,c
b. S,b
c. S,a
d. S,e

SECTION 2

2.1 teacher, parent, or helper check

2.2 within his own experience

2.3 a character whose traits are
borrowed from many people.

126

2.4 a. write what is meaningful to
         you
     b. write what you know

2.5 a. Example:
         Love can triumph over hatred.
     b. Example:
         Temperance is wiser than
         indulgence.

2.6 self check

2.7 Hint:
     Avoid strung together adjectives.
     Place most striking detail first
     and most significant detail last.

2.8 teacher check

2.9 teacher check

2.10 Example:
         "I don't want to go Mother,"
     Tommy said, "What difference does
     Brenda's graduation make to me?"
         "She'll be terribly disap-
     pointed if you don't, dear,"
     Mother replied calmly.
         "Oh, Mom! It will be boring.
     He'll say it's the best class
     ever, the same thing he says
     every year. What a drag!"
         "You're going Tommy,"
     Mother said. "And that's final."

2.11 teacher check

2.12 a. his own
     b. any character's

2.13 a. narration
     b. both

2.14 yes

2.15 the boy
     He is tall and thin; he has long
     fingers, trembling hands and pale,
     gleaming cheeks; his eyes are grey
     and troubled.

2.16 Jim's

2.17 Jim's

2.18 Hint:
     If the omniscient point of view is
     used, thoughts must be provided
     for the boy. If the dramatic
     point of view is used, Jim's
     thoughts and feelings must be
     eliminated. If the personal
     point of view is chosen, the refer-
     ences to Jim must be changed to
     first-person pronouns.

2.19 The personal point of view, be-
     cause the personal point of view
     covers the same range of thoughts
     and feelings as the limited omni-
     scient viewpoint.

2.20 a. the dramatic point of view
     b. the personal point of view

2.21 The writer can reveal the thoughts
     of all characters.

2.22 Example:
     The reader may be unable to decide
     where his sympathies should lie.

2.23 student check

2.24 a

2.25 a

2.26 b

2.27 Example:
     Monica got out of the car and
     walked toward the house. She
     kicked the snow off her boots be-
     fore she went inside.

2.28 a. Example:
         Cathy Miller, active in church
         and Honor Society
     b. Example:
         Harold Kirkpatrick, 52, Cathy's
         boss, businesslike, brusque
     c. Example:
         the Rev. Willis Reed, 34,
         concerned, patient, kind

2.29 Example:
     Cathy finds a job in a bookstore.
     She sees another clerk stealing
     money but says nothing. She is
     accused of the theft and fired.
     When the money is "found" and
     Cathy gets her job back, she is

rude to the other clerk, but when
the other clerk offers to tell
the truth, Cathy follows her
minister's advice and forgives
her.

2.30 Example:
A Christian forgives others for
their sins against him.

2.31 teacher check

SECTION 3

3.1 Zacharias

3.2 a hymn of praise

3.3 Example:
His dumbness was cured after he
saw his child and named him John
(see Luke 1:5-22).

3.4 a. Example:
the bell-like clang of pan
lids
b. Example:
a wispy child, transparent
as a leaf
c. Example:
light as a leaf on the wind

3.5 Example:
Charity is a lovely woman with
serene eyes and a gently smiling
mouth. Her smooth hands are
always extended to help the poor,
a child, an animal, or anyone
in need.

3.6 Example:
The blowing of the trumpet
drowned out the shrill squawking
of the woodwinds except for one
squealing clarinet and a trilling
piccolo. In the background the
bass drum rumbled ominously.

3.7 Example:
Lemon drops are worth more to me
than love or money.

3.8 a. Example:
Like a thief in the night,
the silent snake slithers
through an unnoticed crack
in the garden wall.

b. Example:
alliteration: "s" in silent,
snake, slithers;
assonance: "i" in like, night,
silent;
consonance: "k" in like, snake,
crack

3.9 Hint:
See the example in the text. The
first line should contain nothing
but the name. Be sure the rhyme
scheme is aabb.

3.10 Examples:
a. Jenny has a lovely smile.
b. I wish that I would fall
asleep.
c. for the smell of the sea is
as salt as the taste

3.11 Example:
The sunset paints a watercolor
sky; Dusk washes it away before
it's dry.

3.12 Example:
The people are not individuals but
symbols of universal man.

3.13 Hint:
See the sample in the text.

3.14 a. The same two lines are alter-
nated in the tercets and used
together in the quatrain.
(One of these is also the
first line of the poem.)
b. iambic pentameter

3.15 thirteen lines with two rhymes
The opening words are repeated
twice as an unrhymed refrain.

3.16 a. a narrative poem with short
stanzas and often a refrain
(variation of ballade)
b. three stanzas of eight or ten
lines each and an envoy of
four or five lines; the last
line of each stanza and of the
envoy is the same
c. the closing stanza of a
ballade

3.17 Example:
If slant rhymes such as wordless
and birds are counted as rhymes,
the rhyme scheme is approximately
aa, bb, cc, dd, ee, fff, eee, gg,
hh, ij, kj. The meter is non-
existent.

3.18 teacher check

3.19 shadow mountains

3.20 It refers to the flood of
Noah's time.

3.21 Example:
Ghosts of mountains submerged
during Noah's Flood, many ages
ago.

3.22 metaphor, simile, personification

3.23 personification (also implied
metaphor)

3.24 alliteration, assonance, consonance,
onomatopoeia

3.25 teacher check

1.1 false

1.2 true

1.3 false

1.4 false

1.5 true

1.6 a. rural or agricultrual
b. urban or industrial

1.7 factories

1.8 working

1.9 representation

1.10 a. reform
b. revolt

1.11 Any order:
a. leisure time
b. education
c. cultural pursuits
or material goods

1.12 For the first time in English history, the right to vote was granted to the middle class.

1.13 Verse 40 and Verse 45 ". . . Inasmuch as ye have done it unto one of the least of these my brethren, ye have done it unto me." and ". . . Inasmuch as ye did it not to one of the least of these, ye did it not to me."

1.14 a. NC
b. NC
c. R
d. NC
e. NC
f. R
g. NC
h. R
i. R
j. NC

1.15 The pantheist does not see God as a separate Being that exists outside of nature or the universe. All elements of the universe equally share in the essence of God, but God is not separate from them. The Christian believes in God as a distinct Being in Himself. Nature is a manifestation, a symbol, of His beauty and power; but it is not equal to Him.

1.16 a. NC
b. R
c. NC
d. R
e. R
f. R
g. R
h. NC

1.17 b

1.18 b

1.19 a

1.20 b

1.21 d

1.22 c

1.23 A common subject of romantic poetry is the individual poet himself: his experiences, his emotional reactions, and his feelings. The poems are often written in the first person. Romantic poets believed that their positions as individuals made their subjectivity justifiable.

1.24 In the objective approach the poet presents what is. In the subjective approach the poet presents what exists as he sees it.

1.25 false

1.26 false

1.27 true

1.28 false

1.29 true

1.30 false

1.31 Wordsworth indicated that the commonplace should be colored by the imagination to show that in even the most trivial elements of life, one can find wonder.

1.32 false

1.33 true

1.34 false

1.35 false

1.36 true

1.37 true

1.38 false

1.39 true

1.40 hard working; persevering in doing work conscientiously

1.41 conformity with what is fitting and proper with accepted standards of behavior

1.42 a

1.43 b

1.44 b

1.45 c

1.46 b

1.47 c

1.48 b

1.49 a

1.50 helper check

1.51 eighteen years old

1.52 sixty-four years

1.53 the ability to judge soundly and act sensibly

1.54 to fill (the mind); to inspire

1.55 the virtues of piety and proper social conduct

1.56 nine children

1.57 She was a capable sovereign and a dedicated wife and mother.

1.58 teacher check

1.59 c

1.60 e

1.61 b

1.62 a

1.63 f

1.64 a

1.65 d

1.66 true

1.67 false

1.68 false

1.69 false

1.70 true

SECTION 2

2.1 a. 1770
b. 1850

2.2 early

2.3 Any order:
a. the death of his brother
b. the failure of the French Revolution
c. the loss of excitement or alienation from Coleridge; realities of life

2.4 Dorothy

2.5   France

2.6   Lake

2.7   conventional
      or conservative

2.8   Examples:
      a. Wordsworth has returned to
          the scene after five years'
          absence. He sits under a
          sycamore tree and looks
          around. He sees orchards of
          unripe fruit, hedge rows,
          farms, and cottages.
      b. The poet tells how remembering
          this scene has helped him.
          They have brought back to
          him "sensations sweet,"
          influenced his actions, and
          enabled him to better
          understand life.
      c. The poet speaks of the
          frequency with which he
          turned to this scene.
      d. Seeing this area again, the
          poet's mind is revived and
          he hopes that the scene will
          continue to help him in the
          future. He remembers the
          way he felt as a boy, his
          passion. He knows he cannot
          regain the feelings he had
          as a boy, but he can enjoy
          the scenery in a more mature
          manner. He feels now that
          there is something deeper
          in nature, something he did
          not understand before, and
          he knows that nature will
          always be important to him.
      e. Even if he did not feel as
          he did about nature, the
          poet could take comfort in
          the presence of his sister;
          he can see in her the way he
          felt about nature as a young
          man. Again, he talks of
          what nature does for man,
          how it helps him have "lofty
          thoughts" and endure the
          daily routines and trials.

2.9   Any order:
      a. nature as physical beauty
      b. nature as a source of
          emotional comfort,

inspiration, and understanding
      c. nature as a type of divine
          presence

2.10 a. 1
      b. 3
      c. 2
      d. 1
      e. 2
      f. 3

2.11 Example:
      Wordsworth hopes that his sister
      will continue to enjoy the
      external beauties of nature but
      that she will also learn--as he
      did--to treasure the memory of
      these beauties. He hopes that
      the memories of both nature and
      himself will bring her comfort
      later on when she experiences
      "solitude, or fear, or pain, or
      grief." Finally, he hopes that
      she will remember their being
      together in this lovely spot and
      that she will know that her very
      presence made this "green
      pastoral landscape" that he loved
      even dearer to him.

2.12 The imagination colors what the
      poet sees and does not allow a
      separation of the objective from
      the subjective. The changing
      relationship with nature,
      therefore, depends not on nature
      itself, but on the perceiver
      (observer) of nature.

2.13 Wordsworth believed that the
      primary function of poetry is to
      reveal the state(s) of the poet's
      mind.

2.14 Examples; any order:
      a. where the seed fell; Matthew
          13:1-9
      b. tares and the wheat: Matthew
          13:24-30
      c. workers in the vineyard:
          Matthew 20:1-16
      d. growing seeds; Mark 4:26-29
      e. barren fig tree; Luke 13:6-9
      or fig tree as sign of summer;
      Luke 21:29-31, sheep and goats;
      Matthew 25:31-46

2.15 Hint:
Any word(s) that mean "ecstacy" or "extreme joy" are acceptable.

2.16 The second stage: the poet delights in the sensory visual beauty.

2.17 Hint:
Although the man still delights in sensory beauty, he realizes the existence of "natural piety"—perhaps this natural piety is the moral guidance that nature provides for him.

2.18 A person must die in order to live. The truth of this statement is that death is not really the end of life but, instead, is the beginning of eternal life.

2.19 The poet indirectly compares Lucy to a violet half-hidden by a mossy stone.

2.20 The poet directly compares (uses the word "as") Lucy to a single shining star.

2.21 a.
b. X
c. X
d. X
e.
f.

2.22 b

2.23 c

2.24 c

2.25 d

2.26 c

2.27 It is a calm, beautiful evening; the sun is setting.

2.28 She is adoring God.

2.29 the sea

2.30 Seemingly, she is "untouched by solemn thought."

2.31 His daughter is innocent; she is in God's presence. She has not yet experienced the trials of life.

2.32 abba/abba

2.33 abba/acca

2.34 Any order:
a. cde/cde
b. cdc/cdc
c. cde/dce

2.35 a. cdd/ece
b. def/dfe

2.36 The first word—"Milton!"—is trochaic (/⌣) rather than iambic (⌣/).

2.37 true

2.38 true

2.39 false

2.40 false

2.41 false

2.42 false

2.43 true

2.44 a. C
b. W
c. B
d. W
e. C
f. C
g. C
h. B
i. C

2.45 a. Tartary
b. Greece
c. Africa

2.46 a. sight
      b. sight
      c. smell
      d. sight
      e. hearing

2.47 Huge fragments (or rocks) shot out like rebounding hail or like chaffy grain being threshed by a farmer.

2.48 The miracle is the total image created by contrasting sights and sounds. The poet sees the palace atop the hill in the sun and hears the waters rushing in the icy caverns beneath the ground.

2.49 Coleridge presents himself almost as a madman with "flashing eyes" and "floating hair" who causes people to cry "Beware!" Indeed, he is not mad; he, instead, believes he could be so inspired by the "symphony and song" of the damsel that he could, at least in his mind, create sights and sounds as beautiful as the "sunny dome" and "caves of ice."

2.50 alliteration: He repeats the "m" sound in "miles," "meandering, "mazy," and "motion."

2.51 alliteration: He repeats the same initial sound in "Ceaseless" and "seething."

2.52 The repetition of the "m" sound in Line 25 creates a mild, humming effect that is appropriate to a gentle river winding its way through the woods and valleys. The repetition of the "s" sound in Line 17 creates a hissing, explosive effect that is appropriate to the bursting of the fountain.

2.53 assonance: He repeats the long /i/ sound in "twice," "five," "miles," and "fertile."

2.54 He repeats the short /a/ sound in "Xanadu," "Khan," "Alph," "ran, "caverns," and "man." He

repeats a long /a/ sound in "stately" and "sacred." The repetition of the a sounds help establish the soft, dreamlike quality of the poem.

2.55 This rhyme variation is appropriate because it reflects the shifting-- fading in, fading out--effect of the dream.

2.56 Kubla may have found his kingdom engaged in a war.

2.57 a.
      b. X
      c. X
      d.
      e.

2.58 Coleridge was plagued by illness for which he found no cure. Life was often painful to him; perhaps he sometimes felt that life was worse than death.

2.59 Any order:
      a. satire
      b. cynicism
      c. humor

2.60 Byronic hero

2.61 Greece

2.62 Any order:
      a. loved adventure
      b. insisted on freedom of the individual
      c. used himself as subject of his poetry
      d. relied on emotional appeal

2.63 Any order:
      a. larger-than-life
      b. more intense feelings
      c. equaled only by nature
      d. isolated from society
      or powerful; proud; cynical; sad; melancholic; moody; haunted by unidentified and unforgiven sin; turns inward on self; enjoys his suffering

2.64 The Christian believes no sin is unforgivable if the sinner is truly repentant. Rather than torme; himself with guilt, the sinner should confess his sins and trust that God forgives him.

2.65   b

2.66   b

2.67   d

2.68   a

2.69   c

2.70   In Wordsworth's poetry, nature teaches and guides man. In Byron, nature is a companion to the man who is so beyond the average person that only in nature can his passions be equaled.

2.71   It was given to the oldest son of a nobleman before he received his title.

2.72   Both found it meaningless; therefore, they exile themselves from it and seek refuge in the realm of nature.

2.73   He is proud, isolated, dissatisfied with life. He refuses to submit. Only nature is his equal. He is melancholy and desolate.

2.74   They share the same feeling about life and act in the same ways. By creating Childe Harold, Byron increased the quality of his own life and made an image better than himself. Also, the two are blended and mixed together and share many qualities. Usually what Byron says of Childe Harold he also says of himself.

2.75   b

2.76   b

2.77   a

2.78   a

2.79   b

2.80   a

2.81   a

2.82   b

2.83   c

2.84   a

2.85   c

2.86   The poem most heavily relies on Verse 35.

2.87   Byron relies on simile.

2.88   The Assyrians died during the night; they were destroyed by the Angel of Death.

2.89   The Assyrians are like the wolf: vicious, deadly, bloodthirsty. The Jews are like the flock of sheep: gentle, innocent.

2.90   Byron compares alive Assyrians to the summer (green) leaves of the forest. He compares the dead Assyrians to the autumn (withered) leaves of the forest.

2.91   Byron appeals to the sense of sight (reader can see the white foam from the horse's mouth) and to the sense of touch ("cold as the spray" of the ocean).

2.92   The last line alludes to God's power. With only a "glance," God destroys (melts like snow) the enemies of His people.

2.93   In Don Juan, Byron used the iambic meter ($\cup$/). In "The Destruction of Sennacherib" he used the anapestic meter ($\cup\cup$/).

2.94   true

2.95   false

2.96   false

2.97   true

2.98   Any order:
  a. rich, imaginative power
  b. spontaneous melody that reflects the intended mood
  c. beautiful language
  or subjectivity

2.99   Shelley believed love is the source of goodness and truth, the cure for mankind's ills. The Christian believes that God is Goodness and Truth and provides salvation and that God is Love. Unfortunately, Shelley did not recognize God as the source of love.

2.100   d

2.101   e

2.102   a

2.103   b

2.104   c

2.105   c

2.106   a

2.107   b

2.108   a

2.109   a

2.110   b

2.111   c

2.112   b

2.113   a

2.114   a

2.115   a

2.116   a

2.117   a. "tameless"
  b. "swift
  c. "proud"

2.118   Hint:
The West Wind both destroys and preserves. It destroys the old, dead leaves and preserves the new life that is dormant in the seeds underground.

2.119   Like the Christian, the seed must experience a type of death in order to experience meaningful life.

2.120   Both writings express the idea that spring, with its new life, follows winter.

2.121   a b a, b c b, c d c, d e d, e e

2.122   The repeated rhymes link or connect not only the rhymes themselves but also the main idea and images within each section.

2.123   Inspired by a direct, physical contact with the wind, Shelley expresses his love and admiration for the wind and his intense desire to share its strength and creativity.

2.124   The poet most intensely expresses defeat in Section 4: "I fall upon the thorns of life! I bleed!"

2.125   The predominant tone is one of strength and optimism; the poet ends with a trumpet sound of hope: "If winter comes, can spring be far behind?"

2.126   Shelley's point is the social and economic injustice and inequality of nineteenth-century England.

2.127   He tells the men that they gain nothing from their toil; all the profits and benefits go to someone else.

2.128 Shelley compares the poor laborers to working bees (who do all the work) and the wealthy aristocrats to drones (who do no work) who enjoy all the profits.

2.129 Although he sympathizes with the laborers, he cannot accept the fact that they do nothing to free themselves. Therefore, he implies that if they are cowardly enough to enslave themselves ("the chains ye wrought"), they undoubtedly are not brave enough to take the risk of rebelling.

2.130 He seems to have given up hope. Yet, the fact that he is sarcastic with these men he loves—in essence, he says, "Go ahead and kill yourselves"—indicates that he may still hope to jar them into a realistic reaction to their situation.

2.131 An appropriate response would be that peaceful reform is a better solution than violent rebellion. Reform, of course, in reality, is most effective when its necessity is realized and acted upon by the oppressors rather than the oppressed.

2.132 Only the legs of the statue are left standing. The head of the statue is half buried in the sand. The face of the statue shows a frown, a wrinkled lip, and a "sneer of cold command."

2.133 A tyrant, who often tries to make himself immortal, is remembered only for his cruel and ugly image.

2.134 Hint:
Answer should reflect this idea: No one should over-emphasize himself or his position—all will pass away and the world will go on.

2.135 Nothing remains of the "works" of the "king of kings." The statue of the sculptor remains and shall live as long as people read it. Thus, the works of the artists, which discredit Ozymandias, outlive the works and boasts of the tyrant.

2.136 true

2.137 true

2.138 true

2.139 false

2.140 true

2.141 a. X
      b. X
      c.
      d. X
      e. X

2.142 c

2.143 a

2.144 b

2.145 a

2.146 c

2.147 a

2.148 b

2.149 b

2.150 b

2.151 Keats wrote of one of life's most personal experiences: death. Keats knew of death; he had witnessed the death of his mother and brother from tuberculosis and had suspicions that he too had contracted the disease and quite possibly would die before he could fulfill his dreams and goals.

2.152   a.   4
        b.   5
        c.   1
        d.   3
        e.   1
        f.   2
        g.   4
        h.   2

2.153   Example:
        First, Keats compares the urn
        to an "unravished bride"—he
        implies that the urn, unbroken
        and undisturbed, has preserved
        its original purity and
        loveliness. The words
        "unravished bride" could also
        apply to the young maiden in
        Stanza 2 who, though unreached
        by the "fair youth," "cannot
        fade."
        Second, Keats compares the urn
        to the "foster child of silence
        and slow time." The urn is a
        foster child in the sense that
        it is not a natural child: it
        does speak in that it
        communicates to the poet; it
        is not really "of time" because
        it does not fade and decay as
        the years pass.
        Third, Keats compares the urn
        to a "slyvan historian." It
        is a slyvan historian in that
        it speaks of the history of
        the woods, the simple pastoral
        life.

2.154   Music heard by the ear is sweet;
        but music heard by the
        imagination is even sweeter.
        (Keats attributes great power
        to the imagination.)

2.155   The young maiden, though never
        united with her lover in real
        life, will live forever,
        beautiful and fair, on the vase
        and in Keats' poem.

2.156   Works of art (sculpture, poetry)
        bestow immortality on their
        subjects so that the subjects
        can, in a sense, live "forever."

2.157   The scenes on the urn are
        "frozen," unchanging: the fair

youth will never kiss the maiden;
the heifer will never be
sacrificed; the worshipers will
never return to their town. In
real life the characters would
complete their actions and go
on with life. They would,
however, continue to change and
grow older and someday die and
no longer exist in the physical
world.

2.158   Hint:
        Art bestows immortality on the
        beauty of its subject; therefore,
        art presents ideal beauty.

2.159   The beauty of art is truth in
        the sense that it presents and
        preserves the best—the ideal—
        of life as it exists at the
        moment. The statement is not
        true in the sense that it
        ignores the reality—the truth
        —that in real life beauty fades
        and decays with the passing of
        time.

2.160   helper check

2.161   teacher check

2.162   a.   Wordsworth
        b.   Coleridge
        c.   Byron
        d.   Shelley
        e.   Keats

2.163   a.   "Ode on a Grecian Urn"
        b.   John Keats

2.164   a.   *Childe Harold*
        b.   George Gordon, Lord Byron

2.165   a.   "Kubla Khan"
        b.   Samuel Taylor Coleridge

2.166   a.   "Lines Composed a Few Miles
             above Tintern Abbey"
        b.   William Wordsworth

2.167   a.   *Don Juan*
        b.   George Gordon, Lord Byron

2.168   a.   "Ozymandias"
        b.   Percy Bysshe Shelley

3.1 false

3.2 true

3.3 false

3.4 true

3.5 true

3.6 uncertain feelings or conflicting feelings toward someone or something

3.7 It plunged Tennyson into years of grief and the kind of questioning that often accompanies the bewilderment created by death, especially the sudden death of a young person.

3.8 Example:
The poem says that if a person could understand the flower, or any one segment of the universe, no matter how small, he could understand all of life, both natural and supernatural.

3.9 Example:
No. Life is a mystery that cannot be solved but must be lived. Theology can teach a lot about God. The physical and psychological sciences can teach a lot about people. Ultimately, however, studies cannot provide all the answers. One must rely on faith for unexplainable truth.

3.10 b

3.11 a

3.12 b

3.13 c

3.14 b

3.15 a

3.16 c

3.17 a

3.18 a

3.19 b

3.20 b

3.21 teacher check

3.22 false

3.23 false

3.24 true

3.25 true

3.26 e

3.27 c

3.28 a

3.29 b

3.30 He repeats the long /o/ sound to create a sound similar to that of the blowing wind.

3.31 The repetition of the *w* creates the "breathy" sound of the blowing wind.

3.32 He repeats the long /e/ and short /e/ sounds to create a soothing effect.

3.33 Tennyson compares a soul's journey toward God (begun by death) to a ship's voyage (begun by the ship's crossing of the sandbar).

3.34 God

3.35 The poet hopes to see God after he dies.

3.36 In "In Memoriam" Tennyson is tormented by questions and doubts about both life and death. In "Crossing the Bar" he offers evidence that he has resolved his doubts and will die in peace.

3.37 a. 1812
       b. 1889

3.38 dramatic monologue

3.39 Elizabeth Barrett

3.40 psychology

3.41 a. subjectivity
       b.-c. Either order:
       b. idealism
       c. sense of striving for goals

3.42 "Nay, we'll go / Together down, sir."

3.43 the Duchess

3.44 A speaker speaks to a listener who does not verbally respond and in the process reveals a great deal about himself and his wife.

3.45 She did not appreciate his "gift" of family name and heritage (900-year-old name).

3.46 The Duke values art above people and positive human emotions.

3.47 The monologue is dramatic in that, like a drama, it has a definite setting, develops characterization and plot, and creates suspense—how *did* the Duke make all smiles stop? Will he stop the smiles of his next wife?

3.48 a

3.49 b

3.50 a

3.51 Examples; any order:
       a. sight: branch of pear tree almost touches the clover
       b. smell: blossoms and clover
       c. touch: dewdrops
       d. hearing: song of the thrush

3.52 He repeats his song.

3.53 Children can delight in smelling and picking the bright yellow flowers. Also, children might pick them and give them as gifts to others.

3.54 The lark is flying (on the wing).

3.55 Hint:
       January 1 is the beginning of a fresh, new year—life is starting anew as it does in spring. Also, January 1 is like springtime for Pippa. She must work in the factory during April and May and does not have a chance to experience the thrill of springtime that Browning described in "Home Thoughts, from Abroad." Thus, January 1 is Pippa's springtime—a time when she can delight in the dew on the hill, the lark in the sky, the snail on the thorn.

3.56 She is innocent; she is aware of nature; she is trusting—in the goodness of God and, presumably, in the goodness of people.

3.57 This poem illustrates Browning's optimism and idealism—it expresses his confidence in the positive aspects of life. "God's in his heaven—all's right with the world!" are words that have become somewhat of a "trademark" of Browning's optimism.

3.58 b

3.59 c

3.60 f

3.61 d

3.62 a

3.63 Yes, both say love is unselfish, kind, and enduring.

3.64 true

3.65 false

3.66 true

3.67 true

3.68 false

3.69 b

3.70 a

3.71 b

3.72 All these express hope—after the darkness of winter, night, or tragedies of any kind, comes the light of spring, morning, new hope.

3.73 Hopkins presents the Holy Spirit as a large bird, with warm breast and bright wings, that hovers over and cares for the world—just as a mother bird hovers over her brood, her offspring.

3.74 Either order:
a. "like shining from shook foil"
b. "like the ooze of oil crushed"

3.75 Examples:
bright, brilliant, shining, gleaming

3.76 helper check

3.77 Hopkins concludes with a reference to brightness because the Holy Spirit continues to care for a careless world. Thus, a seemingly hopelessly destructive world still has hope.

3.78 abba/abba/cd/cd/cd. The octave follows the traditional scheme; the sestet uses a variation of the traditional scheme.

3.79 The world is charged with the grandeur of God.

3.80 d: "...dearest freshness deep down things"

1.1   Any order:
    a.   bow-wow
    b.   pooh-pooh
    c.   yo-he-ho

1.2   Same order as 1.1:
    a.   First words were imitations of animal cries and natural sounds.
    b.   First words were exclamations of emotion and later were connected with the object or situation of the emotion.
    c.   **Speech began with rhythmic chants of working people or with playing.**

1.3   Either order:
    a.   Indians credit Veracocha, their god and creator, with language.
    b.   Scandinavians believed the gods gave the people the gift of speech.

1.4   Man's brain contains areas for cognitive and motor skills. Man's brain is larger. Man's brain contains areas for nerves that connect to vision, speech, and motor control.

1.5   One country conquered another and imposed its language on the conquered country.

1.6   a.   watch, see
    b.   watch, before

1.7   a.   close by
    b.   close to

1.8   a.   correct, change
    b.   one who changes or corrects

1.9   a.   gather
    b.   act of gathering

1.10 a.   exact words of someone
     b.   capable of using someone's exact words

1.11 true

1.12 false

1.13 **false**

1.14 true

1.15 false

1.16 helper check

1.17 helper check

1.18 a.   F
     b.   F
     c.   0
     d.   F
     e.   0
     f.   0

1.19 teacher or helper check

1.20 teacher check

1.21 Examples:
     a.   How to overcome Fingernail Biting
        The Negative Effects of Overeating
        Self Discipline in My Classroom
     b.   Three Things that Make Me Happy
        The Happiest Moment of My Life
        How to Make Others Happy

1.22 teacher check

1.23 teacher check

1.24 teacher check

1.25 teacher check

1.26 <u>Dad</u> <u>gave</u> (Susan) an (apple.)

1.27 <u>Jane</u> <u>is</u> the smartest (student) in the class.

1.28 <u>Jack</u> <u>played</u> (baseball) after school.

1.29 <u>Tom</u> carefully <u>opened</u> the new (book.)

1.30 <u>Alice</u> <u>rides</u> her (bike) to school almost every day.

1.31 I have no ice cream (in my dish.), prepositional

1.32 (To be a good parent) requires patience., infinitive

1.33 I found my ball (under the lilac bush.), prepositional

1.34 (Running quickly), John caught up to his brother., participial

1.35 (Making decisions) is often difficult., gerund

1.36 I tried and tried (to understand the problem.), infinitive

1.37 We skated (on the frozen lake.), prepositional

1.38 His hobby is (writing poetry.), gerund

1.39 I walked home (after church.), prepositional

1.40 When I eat makes little difference to me., noun

1.41 That you were not injured is fortunate., noun

1.42 Although I wrote three times, I never received an answer., adverb

1.43 Whenever it thunders, I become frightened., adverb

1.44 The suit that I hope to buy is grey., adjective

1.45 The girl who won the contest used to live in my town., adjective

1.46 I was late to class because I overslept this morning.

1.47 When I phoned him, he was not home.

1.48 After I ran three miles, I was tired.

1.49 Although my toast was burned, I ate it anyway.

1.50 I am taller than Jane is.

1.51 fragment

1.52 fragment

1.53 correct

1.54 run-on

1.55 run-on

1.56 dangling modifier

1.57 slang

1.58 vague

1.59 trite

1.60 stilted

1.61 slang

1.62 vague

1.63 trite

1.64 stilted

1.65 teacher check

1.66 self check

1.67 self check

1.68 dialogue

1.69 it is interspersed with ideas that advance the plot

1.70 a. describes character
      b. moves plot forward

1.71 Any order:
      a. omniscient
      b. limited omniscient
      c. dramatic
      d. personal

1.72 a. personal
      b. omniscient
      c. limited omniscient
      d. dramatic

1.73 teacher check

1.74   teacher check

1.75   teacher check

1.76   b

1.77   a

1.78   c

1.79   c

1.80   teacher check

1.81   teacher check

II.   SECTION TWO

2.1   Any order:
    a. manuscripts
    b. drawings
    c. artifacts

2.2   the Celts

2.3   a. Romans
    b-d Any order:
    b. Angles
    c. Jutes
    d. Saxons

2.4   A.D. 597

2.5   Venerable Bede

2.6   Alfred the Great

2.7   a. A.D.1066
    b. Norman Conquest

2.8   i

2.9   e

2.10   a

2.11   c

2.12   j

2.13   b

2.14   g

2.15   f

2.16   d

2.17   "Widsith" is an elegy about a traveling scop: It is probably the oldest poem in English. It describes early tribes and heroes.

2.18   The poet warns that man should not boast of the future and that man should seek God's forgiveness because life is short and glory, vain.

2.19   the sea; it describes the futility of life if man lives only for the things of this world

2.20   the remains of an old Roman city built in England

2.21   a maxim or a short saying; a proverb

2.22   Beowulf is a prince who slays two monsters in his youth. He becomes king of his own land and rules for fifty years. He dies from a wound inflicted by a dragon that he kills. He is burned on a funeral pyre and is buried with the dragon's treasure by the sea.

2.23   Beowulf was said to have been the best, the kindest, and the most courteous ruler in the world. It also says that he desired fame which was one way the Anglo-Saxon believed he could achieve immortality.

2.24   a. Beowulf's loyal retainer who is appointed to succeed him
    b. queen of Denmark
    c. the monster Beowulf slays
    d. king of Denmark
    e. the meadhall

2.25   false

2.26   true

2.27   false

2.28   false

2.29   false

2.30   true

2.31 true

2.32 false

2.33 The Norman language (French and Germanic) influenced Anglo-Saxon resulting in Middle English. Several dialects developed. The southeast Midland dialect, the dialect of London, dominated and led to the development of Modern English.

2.34 It consists of four line stanzas of imabic pentameter. Lines one and three contain four accented syllables; lines two and four have three accented syllables and these two lines rhyme (a, b, c, b).

2.35 Any order:
   a. romance
   b. supernatural things
   c. tragedy
   d. humor
   e. adventure
   f. history

2.36 a. a code of loyalty, honor, courtesy, and bravery for knights of medieval times
   b. the tradition in which the man is wounded by Cupid's arrows when he sees his love: his heart is entered by the arrows, causing him sleeplessness, and so on
   c. lesson teaching

2.37 Any order:
   a. *Sir Gawin and the Green Knight*
   b. *Pearl*
   c. *Piers, Plowman*

2.38 Any order:
   a. *Hous of Fame*
   b. *Book of the Duchesse*
   c. *Troilus and Criseyde*

2.39 Geoffrey Chaucer

2.40 a. tales
   b. framework

2.41 Any order:
   a. chivalry or military
   b. regular clergy
   c. middle class or bourgeoisie

   d. humble Christians
   e. rascals

2.42 d

2.43 a

2.44 g

2.45 h

2.46 c

2.47 i

2.48 e

2.49 b

2.50 He is a self-important rooster with a red comb, black bill, azure legs and toes, white spurs and burnished, golden plummage.

2.51 She is a practical hen, courteous, discreet, and fair.

2.52 He tells her stories about people having dreams that came true. He gives her examples from the Bible and from mythology.

2.53 his pride

2.54 b

2.55 a

2.56 a

2.57 c

2.58 b

2.59 d

2.60 c

2.61 a

2.62 c

2.63 Any order:
   a. Shakespearean (or English)
   b. Spenserian
   c. Petrarchan (or Italian)

2.64 a. fourteen
b. iambic pentameter

2.65 a. abba/abba
b. abab/bcbc/cdcd/ee

2.66 He uses allusion in Line 7. He refers to a god of Greek mythology.

2.67 Any order:
a. time
b. war
c. battles

2.68 The subject will "live" until the end of time. The subject will continue to "live" forever in "this" (the sonnet).

2.69 The images appeal to the sense of sight.

2.70 Not marbel nor the gilded monuments

2.71 abab/cdcd/efef/gg

2.72 Shakespeare wrote this sonnet. Clues to his identity are (1) the Shakespearean sonnet form (Spenser used Spenserian; Sidney used Petrarchan); (2) the theme (time destroys; poetry immortalizes).

2.73 A metaphor compares God to a rock and a fortress.

2.74 a. snow (verse 7)
b. to express contrition

2.75 Example:
As a father forgives and rejoices when his son repents, so too does God forgive and rejoice when His children repent.

2.76 Words not motivated by charity (love) are meaningless.

2.77 Any order:
a. translations
b. essays
c. novellas

2.78 d

2.79 b

2.80 c

2.81 d

2.82 e

2.83 a

2.84 false

2.85 false

2.86 true

2.87 true

2.88 false

2.89 false

2.90 true

2.91 a. 2
b. 5
c. 1
d. 3
e. 4

2.92 false

2.93 true

2.94 false

2.95 a

2.96 b

2.97 c

2.98 a. protects himself (the speech to the court)
b. loved his father; melancholy; delays taking action
c. obedient
d. pompous; politic; deceitful; spying; interested in making a good impression
e. concerned about her son (asks his friends to determine his problem); hasty (her remarriage)

2.99 Any order:
The major conflict is between Hamlet and Claudius. Other conflicts include Hamlet's internal one (his desire to avenge versus his tendency to delay action until he is certain of its correctness); the conflict between Hamlet and Gertrude

(he resents her marriage); the conflict between Hamlet and Ophelia (she has promised not to see him).

2.100   a.   Hamlet sees the ghost for the first time.
        b.   Hamlet passes up the "perfect opportunity" to kill Claudius.
        c.   Hamlet stabs Polonius.
        d.   Hamlet dies. His opponents (Claudius, Laertes, and Rosencrantz and Guildenstern in England) also dies as does his relatively innocent mother.

2.101   teacher check

2.102   Hamlet kills Claudius

2.103   Hamlet's tragic flaw is his inability to make a decision and then carry it out.

2.104   In a sense, Hamlet's conflict is resolved by forces outside him- self. He was forced to kill Rosencrantz and Guildenstern to save his own life. He is also basically forced into a duel (even though logic and Horatio told him he would lose) in which he kills Claudius and he himself dies. Claudius's death, however, was not the result of a deliberate plan of action.

2.105   By medieval standards, Hamlet could (should) avenge his father's death. Christian standards and the system of trial-by-jury would forbid a modern-day Hamlet from seeking revenge.

2.106   e

2.107   g

2.108   h

2.109   a

2.110   d

2.111   f

2.112   b

2.113   i

2.114   false

2.115   true

2.116   true

2.117   false

III.   SECTION THREE

3.1   Any order:

      a.   1629-40, 20,000 Puritans emigrated to New England
      b.   1661, nearly 2,000 clergymen with Puritan leanings were forced to leave the Church of England
      c.   1672, the Test Act required that all government officers take Communion according to the form of the Church of England
      d.   1678, the "Popish Plot," thirty-five Catholics were executed because of the imaginary plot
      e.   1780, London mobs rioted over the extension of Roman Catholic civil rights

3.2   Any order:

      a.   1642-45, the civil war between the Cavaliers and Puritans
      b.   1649, Charles I was executed
      c.   1660, the Restoration
      d.   1688, James II fled England and William and Mary brought the Glorious Revolution
      e.   1701, war with France was declared
      f.   1739, war with Spain was declared
      g.   1756-63, the Seven Years' War
      h.   1789, the French Revolution was begun
      i.   1776, the American Declaration of Independence was signed

3.3   In the 1750s and 1760s, the Industrial Revolution began at which time steam, spinning, and weaving machinery were invented;

trade was expanded as the British Empire became larger.

3.4   1709, the periodical *The Tatler* was established; 1711, the periodical *Spectator* was established

3.5   Charles II

3.6   Laws were being ennacted against them.

3.7   All Tories were dismissed as the Whigs became more powerful.

3.8   It had expanded to include Canada and India.

3.9   b

3.10   c

3.11   a

3.12   d

3.13   b

3.14   c

3.15   b

3.16   b

3.17   d

3.18   c

3.19   An evangelist preaches the gospel.

3.20   The student should use specific examples from the passage to prove that the journey is both literal and symbolic and that the characters, Christian and Evangelist, are both real and symbolic.

3.21   c

3.22   c

3.23   d

3.24   c

3.25   He was an Anglican clergyman.

3.26   the Tories

3.27   Ireland's

3.28   the Lilluputians

3.29   Gulliver's refusal to associate with his family proves that he is unwilling to realize that he himself is human and will remain human.

3.30   a

3.31   b

3.32   acts that reorganized and enclosed land that had once been available to the rural poor

3.33   Wealthy men are not as important to a country as its citizens ("peasantry") on the countryside; once greed drives these citizens away, they will never return.

3.34   Any order:
       a. the French Revolution
       b. the Industrial Revolution in England

3.35   Any order:
       a. nature
       b. supernatural
       c. personal experience
       d. simplicity
       e. individual dignity

3.36   political and economic changes in England

3.37   *Lyrical Ballads* published in 1898 by Wordsworth and Coleridge

3.38   true

3.39   false

3.40   false

3.41   true

3.42   Any order:
       a. description of the physical scene
       b. divine presence
       c. man's changing relationship with nature

3.43 Any order:
a. critic
b. essayist
c. playwright

3.44 Biographia Literaria

3.45 Any order:
a. "Kubla Kahn"
b. "Christabel"
c. "The Rime of the Ancient Mariner"

3.46 mystery or the supernatural

3.47 Answer should mention the Byronic hero—sadness, melancholy, misery; the Byronic hero is stronger and more capable than most. Wordsworth's and Coleridge's views of nature were scenic, supernatural, individual identity. Byron tried to shock readers.

3.48 Any order:
a. "Childe Harold's Pilgrimage"; travelogue
b. "Don Juan"; incidents in Don Juan's life
c. "The Destruction of Sennacherib"; Byron comments on values in life based on Old Testament account

3.49 Shelley was idealistic and believed strongly in what he wrote. Byron often shocked society intentionally.

3.50 A society in which the forces of evil are defeated and love abounds.

3.51 Third rhyme; the first and third lines rhyme and the final sound in the second line establishes the rhyme for the first and third lines in the following stanza.

3.52 The poet's feeling and emotion is evident in the poem.

3.53 true

3.54 false

3.55 true

3.56 false

3.57 true

3.58 Any order:
a. must live in doubt
b. completely reject science
c. abandon their religious faith

3.59 they were not allowed to vote

3.60 a. Mary Ann Evans
b. Charlotte Brontë
c. Emily Brontë

3.61 to expose the inequalities and hypocrisies of the advantaged middle class

3.62 true

3.63 false

3.64 true

3.65 true

3.66 false

3.67 John Stuart Mill

3.68 Shelley

3.69 dramatic monologue

3.70 character and motivation (or psychology)

3.71 poetic drama

3.72 true

3.73 false

3.74 true

3.75 false

3.76 true

3.77 his poetry was not published during the Victorian era

3.78 religious

3.79 sprung rhythm

3.80 actual speech

3.81 the glory of God contrasted by people failing to acknowledge that glory

1.01   Affixes are added to Latin or Greek roots. These affixes are prefixes and suffixes; the addition of suffixes modifies the meaning of the root, creating a new word.

1.02   Any five; any order: technology (food, building trade, firefighting), science (biology, geology, meteorology), literature, music, mathematics

1.03   a commonly used abbreviation (usually the first letter of each word) Acronyms are often used for organizations. Examples: NATO, TVA. Periods are not used after these abbreviations.

1.04   use of one's authority in accord only with one's own will or desire.

1.05   not capable of being called back

1.06   an official public proclamation or order

1.07   act of saying ahead of time

1.08   process of sending out something

1.09   one who leads another away

1.010 act of calling (God) in

1.011 -spect

1.012 -tain

1.013 Trans-

1.014 a. con-
       b. inter-
       c. ad-

1.015 a. -sti-
       b. -voke-

1.016 a. corp
       b. body

1.017 a. fer
       b. to bear/carry

1.018 a. cide
       b. to cut, kill

1.019 a. arch
       b. head, beginning

1.020 a. gam
       b. marriage

1.021 a. gest
       b. to bear

1.022 a. mort
       b. death

1.023 a. nym
       b. name

1.024 d

1.025 f

1.026 e

1.027 g

1.028 b

1.029 a

SELF TEST 2

2.01   ad-; to, toward

2.02   inter; between

2.03   in-; not

2.04   dic-; says

2.05   ver-; turns

2.06   -duc-; leads

2.07   mis-; sent

2.08   -spect; looks

2.09   -able; able

2.010 -tion; act

2.011 -tor; one

2.012 -ness; condition or quality

2.013 A topic sentence is a sentence that states the main idea or subject of a paragraph.

2.014 It is a part of the topic sentence indicating what the paragraph will say about the subject.

2.015 Unity, or oneness, means that everything in a paragraph points in one direction--to the controlling idea.

2.016 Coherence, or flow, means one idea is expressed in a logical, well-organized way. Thought flows from one point to another. Transitions are helpful methods of achieving coherence.

2.017 Manuscript form refers to the appearance of the paper itself--materials used, placement on paper, margins, italics, abbreviation, numbers, and spelling.

2.018 c

2.019 e

2.020 a

2.021 e

2.022 a

2.023 a

2.024 b

2.025 c

SELF TEST 3

3.01 suffix

3.02 prefix

3.03 root

3.04 acronym

3.05 topic sentence

3.06 controlling idea

3.07 coherence

3.08 unity

3.09 sentence fragment

3.010 a dangling modifier.

3.011 Any order:
a. person
b. number
c. gender

3.012 e

3.013 a

3.014 f

3.015 b

3.016 g

3.017 c

3.018 h

3.019 d

3.020 j

3.021 k

3.022 his

3.023 his

3.024 he has

3.025 me

3.026 goes

3.027 Stepping into the mud ruined my shoes.

3.028 While driving, you should pay close attention.

3.029 When I was only eight, my grandfather died.

3.030 Being only three, she was not interested in the play.

3.031 Camping near Lake Clear Water, we caught many fish.

3.032 Examples:
enjoyable, entertaining

3.033   Example;
        an adventure story

3.034   Example:
        went to sleep

3.035   Example:
        very pale, light complected

3.036   Examples:
        good man, honest person

3.037   It serves as an introductory unit -
        a unifying element. It states the
        subject and direction of the paper.
        it is a generalization.

3.038   To find errors in structure, unity,
        grammar, mechanics, or form agree-
        ment, you should proofread in order
        to rewrite your paper correctly
        before giving it to your teacher.

1.01   false

1.02   true

1.03   false

1.04   false

1.05   true

1.06   true

1.07   true

1.08   false

1.09   false

1.010 true

1.011 false

1.012 true

1.013 true

1.014 c

1.015 e

1.016 a

1.017 f

1.018 b

1.019 d

1.020 by adding -ed, -d, or -t to the
       present.

1.021 a. begun
       b. shaken
       c. chosen
       d. done

1.022 past

1.023 subject

1.024 receives the action

1.025 fact or truth

1.026 Either order:
       a. wish
       b. desire

1.027 a. past
       b. present

1.028 receiver

1.029 dependent (subordinate) clauses

1.030 interrogative

1.031 **indefinite**

1.032 a. pronoun
       b. adjective

1.033 Either order:
       a. subject
       b. subject complement

1.034 Either order:
       a. noun
       b. noun substitute
          (pronoun)

1.035 **Either order:**
       a. noun
       b. **pronoun (noun substitute)**

1.036 Either order:
       a. adjective
       b. adverb

1.037 sudden

1.038 connector

SELF TEST 2

2.01   true

2.02   false

2.03   true

2.04   false

2.05   false

2.06   true

2.07   true

2.08   false

2.09   false

2.010 verb (predicate)

2.011 verb

2.012 describes (qualifies)

2.013 Either order:
    a. subject (ive) complement,
    b. object (ive) complement

2.014 Either order:
    a. what
    b. whom

2.015 a. action
    b. linking

2.016 between

2.017 to or for what or whom

2.018 direct object

2.019 after

2.020 an adjective

2.021 noun-verb-noun

2.022 introductory

2.023 behind (after)

2.024 Either order:
    a. subject
    b. predicate

2.025 commas

2.026 a. lain
    b. laid
    c. sat
    d. set

2.027 <u>work effect</u>
    <u>shall be shall be</u>

    (of righteousness)
    (of righteousness)
    peace SC
    quietness SC
    assurance SC

2.028 <u>God</u>
    <u>called</u>

    Israel DO
    wife OC

2.029 <u>God</u>
    <u>gives</u>
    us IO
    support DO

2.030 <u>Son</u>
    <u>is</u>
    (of God)
    Saviour SC

SELF TEST 3

3.01 false

3.02 true

3.03 true

3.04 false

3.05 true

3.06 false

3.07 false

3.08 true

3.09 Any three; any order:
    a. subject
    b. direct object
    c. indirect object
    or subject complement,
    or object of preposition

3.010 Any three; any order:
    a. time
    b. manner
    c. place
    or result, cause, purpose, condi-
    tion, concession, or comparison

3.011 noun

3.012 commas

3.013 participle

3.014 a. sat
    b. set
    c. risen
    d. raised

3.015   Any order:
        a. adjective
        b. adverb
        c. participle
        d. infinitive
        e. adjective clause
        f. adverb clause

3.016   Marcia looked quite different
        although (even though, though)
        her personality had not changed
        at all.

3.017   Put the sizes on the uniforms
        while sorting them out.

3.018   Houses should be designed to take
        advantage of the sun's heat.

3.019   By mistake I opened a package
        addressed to my sister.

3.020   The hero falls in love with a
        countess who is very beautiful.

3.021   Accepting Christ as his Saviour
        changed his entire life.

3.022   My most valuable coin, one from England,
        is worth more than $100.00

3.023   The weather remaining turbulent,
        we will postpone our canoe trip.

3.024   The group, headed by a senior,
        drew up rules for School Spirit
        Week.

3.025   By serving as a popcorn vendor,
        Don saw many good games.

3.026   We walked along the mountain path
        looking for unusual flowers. (Or
        put the participial phrase at the
        beginning of the sentence.)

1.01   eye span

1.02   speaker

1.03   listener

1.04   Any order:
a. visual skill
b. vocabulary
c. purpose for reading
d. mental capacity
   OR
   familiarity with the material
   past experience

1.05   Any order:
a. rapid word indentification
b. rapid phrase identification
   OR
   word meaning

1.06   To improve your eye movement speed, visual perception, and to eliminate the tendency to pronounce orally.

1.07   the subject and what in general will be said about it

1.08   It is the main idea of the paragraph.

1.09   The knowledge of key words with each pattern makes recognition possible and therefore comprehension of the main idea.

1.010   Any order:
a. either or neither
b. similar, dissimiliar
c. nor, but, yet
d. alike, different
e. like, unlike

1.011   Any order:
a. result, reason, why
b. origin, cause
c. effect, consequence
d. because
e. effect

1.012   facts, dates
names, places
specifics that prove the main idea

1.013   a verifiable statement

1.014   an individual emotional response that is not verifiable

1.015   pauses

1.016   implying

1.017   inferring

1.018   topic sentences

SELF TEST 2

2.01   j

2.02   i

2.03   f

2.04   a

2.05   h

2.06   b

2.07   c

2.08   yes

2.09   no

2.010   yes

2.011   yes

2.012   yes

2.013   no

2.014   no

2.015   Contrast

2.016   Example

2.017   Effect

2.018   Analysis

2.019   Division

2.020   What is included in a book and where to find it.

2.021 Section B, page 17

2.022 Index of that section

2.023 An alphabetical listing of words accompanied by their uses and their meanings.

2.024 It contains historical uses of a word and is far more complete than an ordinary dictionary.

2.025 A listing of articles in a large number of popular magazines.

2.026 Consumers' Research

2.027 A listing of names of any particular group and sometimes addresses and telephone numbers.

2.028 a file cataloging all the holdings of a library

2.029 a. title
       b. subject
       c. author

2.030 a. Dewey Decimal system
       b. Library of Congress

SELF TEST 3

3.01 true

3.02 false

3.03 false

3.04 false

3.05 true

3.06 false

3.07 false

3.08 false

3.09 lectures

3.010 100%

3.011 reversed

3.012 had habits previously formed

3.013 are trained

3.014 a. negative
       b. positive

3.015 They are more readable.

3.016 c

3.017 e

3.018 g

3.019 a

3.020 i

3.021 f

3.022 h

3.023 j

3.024 d

3.025 b

3.026 a. call number
       b. title of book
       c. publisher
       d. number of intro. pages
       e. bibliography

3.027 Answers will differ but will list logical facts like — dispensing of news, weather, sports, recipes, advertisements, fashions, etc.

3.028 Actual reading occurs during the pauses.

3.029 greater thought capability
       more adequate speech
       quicker comprehension
       perception

3.030 The use of an author's unique ideas or words without giving proper credit.

3.031 subjects
       title of magazine article
       continuations of articles
       name of magazine
       pages of article

3.032 cause, because, why reason, affect, result, consequence, etc.

3.033   In the topic sentence (usually at the beginning of a paragraph.)

3.034   a. To get actual information accurately.
        b. To list assignments.
        c. To make review easier.
           OR
           To minimize possibility of forgetting.

3.035   Following directions is vital to learning in any field. It includes obedience as a mental attitude.
        One must learn to take direction before he can give it.

3.036   a. Dewey Decimal
        b. Library of Congress

3.037   Some dictionaries are simplified for elementary school use. Some are moderately difficult for average adults. The Oxford English Dictionary is designed for scholarly research.

1.01　true

1.02　false

1.03　false

1.04　true

1.05　true

1.06　true

1.07　true

1.08　true

1.09　false

1.010　Any two; any order:
　　　a.　Attic
　　　b.　Doric
　　or　Achaean

1.011　Alexander

1.012　Any order:
　　　a.　Koiné Greek
　　　b.　Latin
　　　c.　Aramaic

1.013　lateralization

1.014　Veracocha

1.015　Either order:
　　　a.　Ask
　　　b.　Embla

1.016　First words were interjections and exclamations of emotion that became associated with the object that caused the outcry.

1.017　Language originated with rhythmic chants of working adults and playing children.

1.018　words formed in imitation of animal cries and other natural sounds

SELF TEST 2

2.01　h

2.02　e

2.03　j

2.04　a

2.05　c

2.06　d

2.07　b

2.08　g

2.09　i

2.010　f

2.011　Koiné Greek

2.012　Any order:
　　　a.　angular gyrus
　　　b.　limbic system
　　　c.　lateralization

2.013　Any order:
　　　a.　semantic fallacy
　　　b.　logical fallacy
　　　c.　normative fallacy

2.014　Hebrew

2.015　Any order:
　　　a.　noun
　　　b.　verb
　　　c.　adjective
　　　d.　adverb
　　　e.　auxiliary
　　　f.　preposition
　　　g.　determiner
　　　h.　conjunction
　　　i.　pronoun
　　　j.　interrogative
　　　k.　intensive
　　　l.　"empty words"

2.016　Example:
that the god Veracocha, who created them, gave them the gift of language

2.017 Example:
The gods created a man and a woman from two trees, an ash and an elm, and gave their creations the gift of language.

2.018 Example:
After Philip of Macedonia conquered Greece, the Attic dialect of Athens mingled with other dialects, creating a common tongue called Koiné. Koiné Greek was spread throughout the known world by Philip's son, the conqueror Alexander.

SELF TEST 3

3.01 c

3.02 h

3.03 e

3.04 g

3.05 i

3.06 b

3.07 j

3.08 d

3.09 a

3.010 f

3.011 false

3.012 true

3.013 false

3.014 true

3.015 false

3.016 true

3.017 false

3.018 false

3.019 true

3.020 false

3.021 structural linguistics

3.022 semantikos

3.023 changes in form

3.024 Latin

3.025 common

3.026 advertising

3.027 a. formal
b. frozen
c. casual

3.028 connotation

3.029 friends

3.030 Hint:
business associates or teachers, parents

3.031 a

3.032 b

3.033 b

3.034 a

3.035 c

3.036 a

3.037 c

3.038 c

3.039 b

3.040 a

3.041 literary

3.042 study of word meaning

3.043 semantikos, signification

3.044 transformational grammar

1.01   Any order:
a. Early Britons
b. Celts
c. Romans
d. Anglo-Saxon (and Jutes)
e. Danes

1.02   a. inflection
b. gender

1.03   scop

1.04   alliteration

1.05   kenning

1.06   epic

1.07   Grendel

1.08   true

1.09   false

1.010   true

1.011   false

1.012   true

1.013   true

1.014   false

1.015   false

1.016   true

1.017   false

1.018   a

1.019   d

1.020   b

1.021   a

1.022   a

1.023   e

1.024   repetition of initial sound in two or more words.

1.025   portion of England ceeded to Danes to keep peace.

1.026   king who died at beginning of Beowulf - came from sea - sea burial

1.027   king of Danes

1.028   fame, man's deeds and goodness live on after him

1.029   outside comitatus, has no place, no protection, no Lord

1.030   Widsith

1.031   Any order:
a. Hrothgar and his men
b. Beowulf and his men
c. Geats and Danes
d. Beowulf and his uncle or Beowulf and Wiglaf

SELF TEST 2

2.01   Hrothgar

2.02   Stonehenge

2.03   the Danelaw

2.04   Thomas à Becket

2.05   Either order:
a. trade
b. growth of manufacturing or industry

2.06   friars

2.07   b

2.08   d

2.09   a

2.010   c

2.011   h

2.012   e

2.013   i

2.014   f

2.015   long narrative poem about national hero

2.016   a double metaphor

2.017   a repetition of initial sounds in two or more words

2.018   anonymous dramatic song passed on through oral tradition

2.019   poet at court or traveling poet

2.020   Any order:
a. "The Wanderer"
b. "The Ruin"
c. "The Seafarer"

2.021   a. William
b. William II
or Henry Beauclerc

2.022   a. church
b. feudalism

2.023   a. epic
b. gnomic verse
c. riddle

2.024 Any order:
a. **Norman-French influence,** French influence
b. French and Latin spoken officially and by upper classes
c. English spoken by the lower class
d. literature in three languages French words or matters of government, art, and learning entered the language.

2.025 Geoffrey of Mammouth

2.026 **It was written in Latin.**

2.027 A long poem written by Layamon about the History of Britain tracing the history back to Troy and a hero, Brut, who supposedly founded England.

2.028 Anglo-Saxon

SELF TEST 3

3.01 Canterbury Tales

3.02 **representative of the society of the day**

3.03 Any order:
a. Chaucer
b. Langland
c. Gower

3.04 alliteration

3.05 Any order:
a. Prioress
b. Monk
c. Friar
or Second nun
   Nun's Priest

3.06 1066

3.07 oral tradition

3.08 a. fabliau
b. Mock-heroic

3.09 d

3.010 f

3.011 b

3.012 e

3.013 a

3.014 c

3.015 Any order:
a. inflation
b. warfare (weapons)
c. growth of cities
d. social dissatisfaction

3.016 Any order:
a. Nun's Priest's Tale
b. Pearl
c. Hous of Fame
d. Parliment of Foules
or Book of Duchesse
   Piers Plowman

3.017 Form of literature in which the poet falls asleep in a meadow or wood and has a dream or vision. Device used to tell a story, usually an allegory, within a story.

3.018 humorous tale popular in French literature

3.019 literary form that treats trivial matters in an epic style

3.020 relationship between king and his retainers or witan in Anglo-Saxon times

3.021 a

3.022 c

3.023 b

3.024 c

3.025 b

3.026 c

3.027 a

3.028 c

3.029 d

3.030 b

3.031 Norman-French influenced by Germanic

3.032 Lowest person, bound to the land and to the manor

162

1.01   d

1.02   a

1.03   b

1.04   e

1.05   c

1.06   something not concrete, quality separated from an object

1.07   something than can be perceived by one or more of the five senses

1.08   to give lasting fame to something or someone

1.09   a figure of speech which compares two very dissimilar things

1.010 d

1.011 b

1.012 c

1.013 a

1.014 fourteen

1.015 iambic pentameter

1.016 parable

1.017 Francis Bacon

1.018 false

1.019 false

1.020 true

1.021 false

1.022 true

1.023 Any order:
  a. Italian (or Petrarchan) sonnet
  b. Spenserian sonnet
  c. English (or Shakespearian)
  d. All the sonnets have 14 lines and are written in iambic pattern. They differ in their rhyme schemes.

1.024 Psalm comes from a Greek word that literally meant a pulling or twanging with the fingers.

1.025 An epistle is a letter. In the New Testament, epistles identify the letters the disciples sent to the early Christian communities.

1.026 petition; contrition; praise; thanksgiving

1.027 Line 7—refers to Mars, Greek god of war

1.028 a. time
       b. war
       c. battles

1.029 The subject will "live" until the end of time.

1.030 The subject will "live" in "this" (the sonnet).

1.031 nŏt mȧrblĕ nór thĕ guildĕd mónŭméńts

1.032 abab/cdcd/efef/gg

1.033 a poet can immortalize love and beauty in his poetry

1.034 sense of sight

SELF TEST 2

2.01   3

2.02   4

2.03   2

2.04   1

2.05   d

2.06   a

2.07   b

2.08	b		2.037	Spenser of Sidney
2.09	d		2.038	psalm
2.010	e		2.039	g
2.011	c		2.040	d
2.012	false		2.041	b
2.013	false		2.042	f
2.014	false		2.043	h
2.015	true		2.044	e
2.016	false		2.045	c
2.017	false		2.046	a
2.018	false		2.047	III
2.019	true		2.048	1
2.020	false		2.049	3
2.021	true		2.050	2
2.022	false		2.051	4
2.023	false		2.052	I
2.024	true		2.053	1
2.025	false		2.054	4
2.026	false		2.055	2
2.027	Everyman		2.056	3
2.028	fourteen		2.057	IV
2.029	iambic pentameter		2.058	4
2.030	Lord Chamberlain's Men		2.059	1
2.031	imagery		2.060	3
2.032	the Globe		2.061	2
2.033	Stratford		2.062	V
2.034	groundlings		2.063	2
2.035	personification		2.064	3
2.036	soliloquy		2.065	1

2.066   5

2.067   4

2.068   II

2.069   1

2.070   4

2.071   2

2.072   3

2.073   out of its proper historical time

2.074   relieving or cleansing of emotions by art

2.075   repetition of initial consonant sounds

2.076   indirect comparison (does not use like or as)

2.077   reference to someone or something well known

2.078   a short fictitious story that teaches a lesson

2.079   Any order:
   a.   A tragedy ends in an unhappy catastrophe, usually with the death or destruction of the hero.
   b.   The final disaster is neither contrived nor an accident; it results from the hero's tragic flaw.
   c.   Both playwright and audience consider the account serious.

2.080   a.   exposition: provides intro- duction to characters, setting, and background information.
   b.   rising action: the part of a tragedy that builds suspense as the hero encounters conflicts and gains control over his oponent.
   c.   climax: the turning point of the play.
   d.   falling off: follows climax and portrays various stages in hero's downfall.

   e.   catastrophe: the conclusion which show's the hero's destruction.

2.081   Hamlet's tragic flaw was his inability to take action on his decisions. This inability created a conflict with his strong desire to kill Claudius as an act of revenge. He finally did kill Claudius but not as a result of definite plan of action.

SELF TEST 3

3.01   false

3.02   false

3.03   true

3.04   true

3.05   false

3.06   false

3.07   true

3.08   false

3.09   true

3.010   true

3.011   h

3.012   d

3.013   f

3.014   g

3.015   c

3.016   a

3.017   b

3.018   interpretation

3.019   Either order:
   a.   dialogue
   b.   soliloquies

3.020   evidence or support

3.021 church

3.022 exposition

3.023 Horatio

3.024 Polonius

3.025 too broad

3.026 X

3.027 X

3.028 too broad

3.029 too broad

3.030 X

3.031 X

3.032 to teach a religious lesson

3.033 to amuse or entertain

3.034 to instruct people in the liturgy

3.035 to "cleanse" or relieve the emotion

3.036 to specify, in a sentence, the topic of a critical essay

3.037 Hamlet procrastinated about avenging his father's death.

3.038 Any order:
  a. Interpretation answers, "What did the writer say?"
  b. Analysis answers, "How did he say it?"
  c. Evaluation answers, "What is the worth of his saying it?"

3.039 Detailed evidence determines the worth of an interpretation.

3.040 a. The main external conflict is the tension between Claudius and Hamlet.
  b. The major internal conflict is the tension created within Hamlet by his tendency to think rather than act and his desire to kill Claudius.

3.041 a. The exciting force is the appearance of the Ghost to Hamlet for the first time at the end of Act I.
  b. The climax is Hamlet's passing up his opportunity to kill Claudius. (Some critics believe the climax is Hamlet's stabbing of Polonius - this answer is also acceptable).
  c. The catastrophe occurs in the final scene with the death of Hamlet and those who die with him.

1.01   c

1.02   b

1.03   a

1.04   b

1.05   a

1.06   d

1.07   b

1.08   d

1.09   c

1.010   c

1.011   a. laws
        b. Parliament
        c. Charles I

1.012   a. James II
        b. Holland
        c. Parliament

1.013   a. newly industrialized areas
        b. slums (or poverty)

1.014   a. the Classics (or a university
           education)
        b. periodicals

1.015   They believed that the Anglican
        Church was corrupted by unneces-
        sary ritual and an organization
        that was no longer able to reach
        each member, and was controlled
        by a corrupt government and
        monarchy.

1.016   The Whigs and Tories fought for
        political control of Parliament;
        the Tories were critical of
        William's military policies.

1.017   More jobs were available in cities
        and areas where there were fac-
        tories. The poor came to these
        areas to find work, and the owners
        and white-collar workers of those
        factories prospered.

1.018   The authors writing in the period
        of Common Sense believed that
        their work should be (a) reason-
        able; (b) realistic; (c) without
        excessive religious emotions which
        seemed false or boastful; and
        (d) critical of the way life is
        being lived to correct bad prac-
        tices and encourage good ones.

1.019   a. emotional
        b. lyrical
        c. emphasis on common man
        d. interest in supernatural ele-
           ments
        e. interested in beauties of
           nature
        or emphasis on distant past;
           probed the effects of melanchol

1.020   false

1.021   false

1.022   false

1.023   false

1.024   false

1.025   false

1.026   true

1.027   true

1.028   true

1.029   false

SELF TEST 2

2.01   false

2.02   true

2.03   true

2.04   true

2.05   true

2.06   false

2.07   false

2.08   true

2.09   true

2.010   false

2.011   f

2.012   k

2.013   g

2.014   j

2.015   b

2.016   a

2.017   d

2.018   e

2.019   i

2.020   h

2.021   c

2.022   c

2.023   b

2.024   a

2.025   d

2.026   b

2.027   b

2.028   c

2.029   b

2.030   c

2.031   rhyme

2.032   sonnet

2.033   personification

2.034   obey

2.035   alliteration

2.036   a. his mother's death
        b. his friend's death
        c. his Puritan background
        d. his wives' deaths
        e. his blindness
        or his political writing
            his imprisonment

**2.037   The main idea is that Christ gave
        up his comfortable position in
        heaven to live as a man on the
        earth, and that he drove away
        evil and false teachings (that he
        came to the earth).**

2.038   Not everyone has to be active to
        do God's will.

2.039   They are all examples of "one
        just man," a man whose goodness
        prevents God from destroying all
        men.

2.040   If you gain all these things, you
        will be at peace with yourself.

2.041   They are described with realistic
        details that allows the reader to
        see and hear — and, therefore,
        feel with — the characters.

SELF TEST 3

3.01   true

3.02   false

3.03   false

3.04   true

3.05   true

3.06   true

3.07   true

3.08   false

3.09   true

3.010 false

3.011 c

3.012 f

3.013 d

3.014 a

3.015 e

3.016 d

3.017 a

3.018 a

3.019 c

3.020 b

3.021 d

3.022 c

3.023 b

3.024 a

3.025 b

3.026 epic

3.027 allegory

3.028 commonwealth

3.029 symbol

3.030 personify

3.031 Brobdingnagians

3.032 realistic details

3.033 types of people

3.034 undignified

3.035 insects or vermin

3.036 a. The Drapier's Letters
       b. A Modest Proposal

3.037 Adam is willing because he has

seen Christ's future redemption and because he has learned how to gain a "paradise within."

3.038 He represents a man trying to overcome inner obstacles to save his soul.

3.039 He criticizes trade, wars, political and religious disagreements, and professional positions, all problems of Swift's England.

3.040 A flapper is necessary because their minds are usually so absorbed in abstract thought that they are unable to carry on their daily lives without the attention-getting instruments.

3.041 His repulsion shows that Gulliver is so repulsed by mankind that he is unable to feel warmth, that he has been driven mad by self-hate.

SELF TEST 4

4.01 true

4.02 true

4.03 false

4.04 true

4.05 false

4.06 true

4.07 false

4.08 true

4.09 true

4.010 false

4.011 false

4.012 d

4.013 c

4.014 a

4.015 d

4.016   c

4.017   b

4.018   a

4.019   c

4.020   a

4.021   b

4.022   sonnet

4.023   simile

4.024   alliteration

4.025   allegory

4.026   heroic couplet

4.027   irony

4.028   satirizing

4.029   Tory

4.030   Enclosure

4.031   sentimentality, emphasis on emotions

4.032   poetic diction

4.033   c

4.034   d

4.035   b

4.036   Any order:
a. the Civil War
b. the Commonwealth
c. the Restoration
d. the Test Act of 1672
e. the Glorious Revolution
or the Industrial Revolution
    the Enclosure Acts
    expanding trade
    wide-spread education
    an enlarged British Empire

4.037   Because he has seen Christ's future redemption, and because he has learned how to gain a "paradise within."

4.038   They are described with realistic details.

4.039   **Either order:**
a. He wrote for the Tories.
b. He was an Anglican clergyman.
or He wrote for Irish rights.

4.040   a. The village is deserted because a lord has bought the land and turned the villagers away.
b. The villagers must now go to crowded, corrupted cities, or to America.
c. The poet emphasized the loss by saying that he himself had planned to retire there.

1.01 true

1.02 true

1.03 false

1.04 false

1.05 false

1.06 e

1.07 h

1.08 d

1.09 g

1.010 b

1.011 i

1.012 a

1.013 c

1.014 d

1.015 c

1.016 a

1.017 Hint:
Answer should indicate that internal conflict involves forces within a character's mind, e.g. desire vs. responsibility. **External conflict occurs between** a character and someone or something else, e.g. man vs. nature or conflict of wills.

1.018 Example:
a character seen only from the outside, through words and actions

1.019 Example:
a character whose attitude, etc. is shaped in part by the events in his life

1.020 Example:
the emotional quality that pervades and colors a poem or story

1.021 emotional

1.022 images

1.023 slant rhyme

1.024 a. anapestic
b. dactylic

1.025 tetrameter

1.026 h

1.027 g

1.028 e

1.029 c

1.030 a

1.031 b

1.032 d

1.033 b

1.034 b

1.035 c

1.036 d

SELF TEST 2

2.01 theme

2.02 iamb

2.03 paradox

2.04 denouement

2.05 personal or first person

2.06 true

2.07 false

2.08 true

2.09 false

2.010 false

2.011   e

2.012   g

2.013   f

2.014   i

2.015   c

2.016   b

2.017   j

2.108   k

2.019   d

2.020   a

2.021   hyperbole

2.022   personification

2.023   metaphor

2.024   apostrophe

2.025   paradox

2.026   simile

2.027   b

2.028   e

2.029   c

2.030   a

SELF TEST 3

3.01   b

3.02   d

3.03   a

3.04   a

3.05   a

3.06   b

3.07   d

3.08   b

3.09   d

3.010   a

3.011   iambic tetrameter

3.012   anapestic trimeter

3.013   trochaic tetrameter

3.014   iambic trimeter

3.015   dactylic dimeter

3.016   occasional

3.017   assonance

3.018   onomatopoeia

3.019   clerihew

3.020   parody

3.021   a. Shakespearian
        b. Petrarchan

3.022   quatrain

3.023   metonymy

3.024   apostrophe

3.025   false

3.026   false

3.027   false

3.028   false

3.029   false

1.01 a. political c. philosophical
      b. Industrial d. poetic

1.02 R

1.03 NC

1.04 NC

1.05 R

1.06 NC

1.07 NC

1.08 R

1.09 R

1.010 R

1.011 NC

1.012 NC

1.013 R

1.014 R

1.015 NC

1.016 NC

1.017 NC

1.018 R

1.019 NC

1.020 NC

1.021 R

1.022 b

1.023 c

1.024 c

1.025 d

1.026 a

1.027 true

1.028 false

1.029 false

1.030 true

1.031 false

1.032 true

1.033 true

1.034 true

1.035 true

1.036 false

1.037 b

1.038 d

1.039 c

1.040 e

1.041 f

1.042 Any order:
       a. individualism
       b. nature
       c. emotion
       d. simplicity
       e. imagination
       f. mystery

1.043 Examples:
       Thomas Carlyle, Thomas Babington
       Macaulay, Matthew Arnold, John
       Henry Newman, John Ruskin

1.044 Charles Dickens

1.045 William Makepeace Thackeray

1.046 Mary Ann Evans or George Eliot

1.047 Brontë

1.048 In the Victorian Age, the poet
       needed to be purposeful. As a
       prophet or a teacher, his role
       was to help improve his society.

The romantic poet was primarily concerned with expressing his own ideas, feelings, and emotions.

SELF TEST 2

2.01   false

2.02   true

2.03   true

2.04   true

2.05   false

2.06   c

2.07   h

2.08   d

2.09   b

2.010 a

2.011 i

2.012 e

2.013 f

2.014 c

2.015 c

2.016 b

2.017 c

2.018 b

2.019 b

2.020 b

2.021 c

2.022 a

2.023 b

2.024 e

2.025   a. "Ode to a Grecian Urn"
        b. John Keats

2.026   a. from *Childe Harold*
        b. Lord Byron

2.027   a. "Kubla Khan"
        b. Samuel Taylor Coleridge

2.028   a. "Ode on a Grecian Urn"
        b. John Keats

2.029   a. "Tintern Abbey"
        b. William Wordsworth

2.030   a. "Ode to the West Wind"
        b. Percy Bysshe Shelley

2.031   alliteration
        or assonance

2.032   imagery

2.033   "Ozymandias"

2.034   the Oxford Movement

2.035   novel

2.036   contrast
        or conflict

2.037   melancholy
        or sadness

2.038   a. reason
        b. emotion
        c. artificiality
        d. simplicity
        e. Greek
        f. medieval
        g. rules and restrictions
        h. freedom and spontanaeity
        i. social status
        j. individual
        or urban, rural
        analysis, synthesis (meditation
        and intuition)

2.039   Any order:
        a. material poverty: The poor
            barely existed and the
            working class frequently
            lived and worked in inhumane
            conditions.

b. political poverty: Unable to vote, the lower classes had to depend on others for help.

c. spiritual poverty: The industrial and scientific progress created a sense of materialism and doubt that shook or destroyed a spiritual basis for living. The Anglican Church provided little guidance.

SELF TEST 3

3.01 false

3.02 false

3.03 true

3.04 false

3.05 true

3.06 true

3.07 c

3.08 c

3.09 b

3.010 b

3.011 b

3.012 c

3.013 a

3.014 d

3.015 a

3.016 b

3.017 e

3.018 d

3.019 a

3.020 c

3.021 b

3.022 Arthur Hallam

3.023 John Keats

3.024 Samuel Taylor Coleridge

3.025 William Wordsworth

3.026 George Gordon, Lord Byron

3.027 Percy Bysshe Shelley

3.028 George Gordon, Lord Byron

3.029 a. "God's Grandeur"
     b. Gerard Manley Hopkins

3.030 a. "My Last Duchess"
     b. Robert Browning

3.031 a. "Crossing the Bar"
     b. Alfred, Lord Tennyson

3.032 a. "Sonnet 43"
     b. Elizabeth Barrett Browning

3.033 Tennyson compares a soul's journey toward God (begun by death) to a ship's voyage (begun by the ship's crossing of the sandbar).

3.034 A dramatic monologue is a form of poetry in which only one person speaks to one or more other characters who do not verbally respond. Through his words, the speaker reveals characteristics not only of his own personality, but also of the personalities of the person(s) to whom and/or about whom he is speaking. The monologue is dramatic in that, like a drama, it has a definite setting and develops characterization, plot, and conflict (or suspense).

3.035 Any order:
     a. individualism
     b. emotion
     c. imagination
     d. nature
     e. simplicity

3.036 Any order:
    a. material progress
    b. commercial prosperity
    c. political, social, and
       spiritual poverty
    d. political, social, and
       religious reforms
    e. scientific progress
or a contrast between prosperity
and poverty; conflict between
science and religion; a sense
of doubt; industriousness;
prosperity; Age of the Novel;
sense of morality; temperance;
piety; self-reliance; sincerity

1.01   false

1.02   true

1.03   true

1.04   true

1.05   false

1.06   true

1.07   false

1.08   false

1.09   true

1.010   false

1.011   Either order:
        a.   coherent
        b.   unified

1.012   Either order:
        a.   subject
        b.   predicate

1.013   a.   clauses
        b.   phrases

1.014   **reads groups of words**

1.015   Any order:
        a.   traditional
        b.   structural
        c.   transformational

1.016   Any order:
        a.   simile
        b.   metaphor
        c.   personification
        or apostrophe, irony, paradox,
           metonymy, synecdoche

1.017   Either order:
        a.   meter
        b.   rhyme

1.018   Any order:
        a.   omniscient
        b.   limited omniscient
        c.   dramatic
        d.   personal

1.019   b

1.020   g

1.021   e

1.022   j

1.023   a

1.024   k

1.025   d

1.026   i

1.027   f

1.028   c

1.029   Hiking through canyons is strenuous activity.

1.030   We went ice-skating on the frozen lake.

1.031   This book is an excellent one to read.

1.032   Although it was raining, he decided to walk to school.

1.033   I go to our town library every week.

1.034   The card catalog that is in the reference room gives valuable information about library books.

SELF TEST 2

2.01   true

2.02   true

2.03   false

2.04   false

2.05   true

2.06   false

177

2.07	false	2.036	iambic pentameter
2.08	true	2.037	Spenser or Sidney
2.09	true	2.038	The Globe
2.010	true	2.039	Bede
2.011	c	2.040	Southeast Midland

2.041 Any order:
   a. Celts
   b. Romans
   c. Danes
   d. Anglo-Saxons and Jutes (Germanic tribes)
   e. Normans

2.012	d
2.013	e
2.014	a
2.015	b
2.016	e

2.042 narration

2.043 Any order:
   a. personal
   b. omniscient
   c. dramatic
   or limited omniscient

2.017	a
2.018	c
2.019	a
2.020	b

2.044 Any order:
   a. chivalric or military
   b. regular clergy
   c. middle class
   d. humble Christians
   e. rascals

2.021	d
2.022	b
2.023	c
2.024	c
2.025	a

2.045 a. exposition
   b. rising action
   c. climax
   d. falling action
   e. catastrophe

SELF TEST 3

2.026	b
2.027	c
2.028	h
2.029	d
2.030	f
2.031	g
2.032	e
2.033	a
2.034	b
2.035	fourteen

3.01	true
3.02	false
3.03	true
3.04	false
3.05	true
3.06	false
3.07	false
3.08	true

3.09   false

3.010   false

3.011   b

3.012   e

3.013   a

3.014   g

3.015   i

3.016   d

3.017   j

3.018   h

3.019   f

3.020   c

3.021   a

3.022   c

3.023   b

3.024   a

3.025   d

3.026   d

3.027   b

3.028   d

3.029   c

3.030   a

3.031   dramatic monologue

3.032   church

3.033   catastrophe

3.034   sprung rhythm

3.035   semantics

3.036   Any order:
    a.   nature
    b.   supernatural
    c.   simplicity
    d.   personal experience
    e.   individual dignity

3.037   Example:
because it is an allegory that deals with a Christian's journey through life to heaven

3.038   His works were not published in the Victorian period.

3.039   Example:
Life is transitory, passing. Things of the world are not as important as things of God.

3.040   Example:
An outline is an organizing structure that helps the writer to see his material, his organization. Serves as a guide to logical, concise writing.

TEST
KEYS

1. true

2. false

3. false

4. true

5. true

6. true

7. false

8. false

9. false

10. true

11. true

12. false

13. true

14. true

15. d

16. m

17. h

18. c

19. i

20. e

21. j

22. a

23. g

24. b

25. to look

26. a. bio
    b. life
    c. graph
    d. to write

27. study of

28. the first letters of a group of words

29. 3rd person, singular, present tense, indicative mood

30. viewpoint

31. Any order:
    a. states, months
    b. countries
    c. days of the week

32. spelled out

33. possessive

34. capitalized

35. is

36. was

37. counts

38. is

39. set, lay

40. his

41. rather

42. many

43. restate the topic sentence or thesis

1. Any order:
    a. adjective
    b. preposition
    c. adverb
    d. noun
    e. pronoun
    f. verb
    g. conjunction
    h. interjection

2. Any order:
    a. adjective
    b. infinitive
    c. adverb
    d. adjective clause
    e. participle
    f. adverb clause

3. Any order:
    a. noun
    b. infinitive
    c. pronoun
    d. noun clause
    e. gerund

4.
    (pro)

    adj   n   conj adj   n   adv adj   n   verb   adv prep adj
    Four score and seven years ago our forefathers brought forth upon this

    n   adj adj   n   v   prep   n   conj   v   prep/adj   n
    continent a new nation conceived in liberty and dedicated to the proposition

    pro adj   n   v   v   adj
    that all men are created equal.

5. beginning—gerund

6. to love—infinitive

7. a. Professing—participle
    b. to be—infinitive

8. understanding—gerund

9. Being justified—participle

10. to be moved—infinitive

11. that sinneth—adjective

12. As many as are led by the Spirit of God—adverb

13. whom God correcteth—adjective

14. what you ought to say—noun DO

15. as the sparks fly upward—adverb

16. that fear Him—adjective

17-25 Examples:

17. The play, a three-act farce, amused everyone.

18. Frances has plenty of time to devote to her painting.

19. Because (since, as) Darla recommended the course, I decided to take it.

20. The two waiters exchanged a look whose meaning was clear to me.

21. The fire jumped across the ditch, threatening our house.

22. The fishing becoming poor, we packed up camp and moved to another lake.

23. Confused by the sign, the driver made the wrong turn. (OR) The driver, confused by the sign, made a wrong turn.

24. Whenever I can come will be soon enough for the race.

25. We hit a snag while rowing to shore.

26. CPD
27. CPX
28. S
29. CPX
30. CPD

1. true

2. false

3. false

4. true

5. true

6. false

7. true

8. false

9. false

10. true

11. true

12. true

13. false

14. true

15. false

16. false

17. true

18. true

19. support details

20. Library of Congress

21. a. books
    b. magazines

22. One has more information upon which to relate new facts.

23. Directory of people equipped to provide services such as — painting, roofing, etc.

24. take notes, pay attention or listen carefully

25. c

26. d

27. f

28. g

29. a

30. j

31. h

32. i

33. e

34. b

35. Readers Guide, card catalogue, encyclopedias, directories, dictionaries, newspaper, microfilm.

36. Taking notes helps one remember material; notes make possible better review; they tend to help one organize main points and subpoints, etc.

37. Any order:
    a. author
    b. title
    c. subject

38. He gets the big picture which makes learning easier; the table of contents is like a map of a journey to which the student relates; the student is more interested by details than by broad generalities, etc.

1. true

2. false

3. true

4. true

5. false

6. false

7. true

8. true

9. true

10. false

11. Either order:
    a. an ash
    b. an elm

12. Veracocha

13. Koiné Greek

14. Any order:
    a. Doric
    b. Attic
    c. Achaean

15. a. "pooh-pooh"
    b. "yo-he-ho"
    c. "bow-wow"

16. a. transform
    b. kernel sentence

17. Noam Chomsky

18. Any one:
    Fries, Sapir, Bloomfield

19. competence

20. paradigm

21. a

22. b

23. b

24. c

25. b

26. c

27. c

28. a

29. b

30. a

31. Hint:
    Semantics is the study of word meanings.

32. A morpheme is a unit of meaning, either a word or an affix.

1. c

2. h

3. b

4. j

5. e

6. a

7. d

8. f

9. m

10. l

11. g

12. n

13. Either order:
    a. kennings
    b. alliteration

14. four

15. 500

16. 1066

17. a. tin
    b. bronze

18. longbow

19. Either order:
    a. the plowman
    b. the parson

20. final "e"

21. Southeast Midland

22. false

23. false

24. false

25. true

26. true

27. false

28. true

29. false

30. He gave us a realistic picture of fourteenth century England. He depicted people from various social classes in a very real way.

31. Changes in language, government and literature. Feudalism was established.

32. Any order:
    a. epics
    b. riddle
    c. elegy
    d. gnome
       or sermon

33. Any order:
    a. histories
    b. sermons
    c. wise sayings
       or Breton lays, lyrics, ballad

34. Any order:
    a. debate
    b. sermons
    c. Breton lay
    d. religious lyrics
    e. didactic
       or secular lyrics, rules for religious tales, or romances

35. Any order:
    a. dream-vision
    b. elegy
    c. religious and moral tales
    d. allegory
    e. fabliau
       or sermons, lay, romances

36. Any order:
    a. towns grew
    b. middle class developed
    c. trade increased
    d. plague struck

1.	false	28.	b
2.	true	29.	h
3.	false	30.	e
4.	true	31.	f
5.	false	32.	a
6.	true	33.	g
7.	false	34.	d
8.	true	35.	c
9.	false	36.	a
10.	false	37.	c
11.	3	38.	b
12.	1	39.	c
13.	6	40.	1
14.	7	41.	4
15.	4	42.	2
16.	5	43.	3
17.	2	44.	climax
18.	i	45.	catastrophe
19.	j	46.	tragic flaw
20.	d	47.	exciting force
21.	k	48.	a. serious
22.	g		b. unhappy
23.	f	49.	evidence
24.	c	50.	soliloquy
25.	b		
26.	e		
27.	h		

1. true

2. **true**

3. false

4. false

5. false

6. true

7. false

8. true

9. false

10. false

11. e

12. g

13. f

14. a

15. h

16. b

17. i

18. c

19. j

20. d

21. d

22. b

23. c

24. a

25. b

26. c

27. d

28. a

29. a

30. d

31. Enclosure

32. cities

33. <u>Gulliver's Travels</u>

34. novel

35. poetry

36. **Adam is willing to leave because he has seen Christ's future redemption, and because he has learned how to gain a "paradise within."**

37. He left Heaven to live in darkness as a mortal.

38. Milton regrets that his blindness restricts his work.

39. It is about a man who saves his soul by overcoming obstacles.

1. Any order:
    a. theme
    b. characterization
    c. plot
    d. setting

2. composite

3. universal

4. d

5. a

6. b

7. e

8. e

9. a

10. b

11. g

12. d

13. c

14. f

15. h

16. a

17. b

18. d

19. a

20. b

21. c

22. e

23. d

24. b

25. i

26. l

27. a

28. h

29. g

30. j

31. f

32. false

33. true

34. true

35. false

36. false

37. false

38. false

39. false

1. true

2. true

3. true

4. false

5. true

6. d

7. e

8. a

9. c

10. Preface

11. Tennyson

12. "Ozymandias"

13. Hopkins

14. "Kubla Khan"

15. Tennyson

16. "Crossing the Bar"

17. h

18. b

19. a

20. j

21. d

22. c

23. k

24. f

25. l

26. g

27. e

28. a

29. a

30. c

31. c

32. a

33. a. "God's Grandeur"
    b. Gerard Manley Hopkins

34. a. "Kubla Khan"
    b. Samuel Taylor Coleridge

35. a. "Ode to the West Wind"
    b. Percy Bysshe Shelley

36. a. "Sonnet 43"
    b. Elizabeth Barrett Browning

37. a. "Tintern Abbey"
    b. William Wordsworth

38. Any order:
    a. doubts about life-after death
    b. doubts about God's providence (concern, care
    c. the conflict between scientific progress and religious faith
    or conflict between God and nature, conflict between elements of nature

39. Any order:
    a. He regards people—especially women—as objects.
    b. He is jealous.
    c. He is proud of himself and his name.
    d. He values art above people and positive human emotion.
    e. He is probably a murderer.
    or He is selfish, cruel, self-centered, greedy
    Hint:
    The five insights should not be redundant.

1. true

2. true

3. true

4. false

5. true

6. false

7. false

8. true

9. true

10. true

11. c

12. b

13. d

14. a

15. e

16. j

17. i

18. g

19. h

20. k

21. l

22. 5

23. 2

24. 4

25. 7

26. 3

27. 6

28. tragic flaw

29. Any order:
    a. personal
    b. omniscient
    c. limited omniscient
    d. dramatic

30. dialogue

31. blank verse

32. terza rima

33. reference to something well known

34. repetition of initial consonant sounds

35. an appeal to the reader's senses

36. a narrative that personifies abstractions

37. events in a story

38. Feudalism is a political system instituted by the Normans to insure loyalty and military support. Land was granted to nobles who granted land to lesser nobles in return for support and loyalty.

39. It is composed of an external framework—a group of pilgrims traveling to Canterbury—and an internal structure—the twenty-four tales told by the pilgrims.

40. Any order:
    a. nature
    b. supernatural
    c. individuality
    d. personal experience
    e. simplicity

1. d

2. j

3. f

4. g

5. b

6. i

7. c

8. a

9. e

10. h

11. true

12. false

13. false

14. true

15. true

16. false

17. true

18. false

19. true

20. false

21. b

22. c

23. d

24. d

25. a

26. Any order:
    a. lingo
    b. jargon

27. acronym

28. parallel constructions

29. colloquial

30. thesaurus

1. Either order:
   a. nouns
   b. noun substitutes

2. concrete

3. modifiers

4. adverb

5. seven

6. Any order:
   a. participles
   b. gerunds
   c. infinitives

7. two

8. Either order:
   a. subject
   b. predicate

9. false

10. true

11. true

12. false

13. true

14. false

15. true

16. false

17. true

18. true

19. Any order:
   a. relative
   b. interrogative
   c. demonstrative
   or reflexive,
      indefinite,
      personal

20. Any order:
   a. present
   b. past
   c. future
   d. present perfect
   e. past perfect
   f. future perfect

21. Any order:
   a. S-V-O
   b. S-V
   c. S-V-Io-Do
   d. S-Lv-N
   or S-Lv-Adj,
      inverted,
      question

22. Any order:
   a. who
   b. whom
   c. whose
   d. which
   or that,
      when,
      where,
      why

23. S-V

24. S-V-Io-Do

25. S-Lv-N

26. S-V-O

27. S-Lv-Adj

1. h

2. c

3. e

4. g

5. d

6. j

7. i

8. b

9. a

10. k

11. true

12. true

13. false

14. false

15. false

16. true

17. false

18. false

19. true

20. true

21. scanning

22. International Standard Book Number

23. directory

24. note card

25. Dewey Decimal

26. plagiarism

27. index

28. *Readers' Guide*

29. process analysis

30. inference

31. topic sentence

32. *Oxford English Dictionary*

33. Any order:
    a. title
    b. author
    c. subject

34. expository

35. c

36. b

37. a

38. d

39. b

40. c

1. true

2. true

3. false

4. false

5. true

6. true

7. false

8. true

9. false

10. false

11. c

12. f

13. e

14. b

15. a

16. d

17. h

18. i

19. k

20. l

21. g

22. m

23. language origin

24. gods

25. Germanic

26. Koiné Greek

27. Alexander

28. Renaissance

29. a. five
    b. three

30. written

31. kernel sentence

32. Greek

33. Example:
    suggested meaning of a word

34. Example:
    division of the cerebrum of the
    human brain into two independent
    halves

35. Example:
    in a constant state of change,
    not stable

36. Example:
    the elements surrounding a
    word that influence its meaning

1. b

2. a

3. d

4. a

5. c

6. b

7. c

8. b

9. a

10. d

11. c

12. e

13. a

14. i

15. b

16. g

17. d

18. j

19. f

20. 1

21. h

22. k

23. false

24. false

25. true

26. true

27. true

28. true

29. false

30. false

31. true

32. true

33. elegy

34. gnomes

35. Domesday Book

36. Any order:
    a. histories
    b. sermons
    c. Breton lays
    or wise sayings, lyrics, ballads

37. feudalism

38. levels or classes or divisions

39. Prologue

40. *The Pearl*

41. King Arthur

42. Either order:
    a. Christian virtue
    b. humility

1. false

2. false

3. true

4. false

5. true

6. true

7. true

8. false

9. false

10. true

11. d

12. f

13. a

14. e

15. b

16. g

17. c

18. i

19. k

20. j

21. m

22. l

23. b

34. a

25. c

26. a

27. d

28. d

29. c

30. a

31. b

32. c

33. Any order:
    a. comedy
    b. history
    c. tragedy

34. personification

35. conflict

36. falling action

37. Either order:
    a. external
    b. internal

38. *Everyman*

39. comic relief

40. Any order:
    a. interpreting
    b. analyzing
    c. evaluating

41. interpretation

42. to discern or separate

1. true

2. false

3. false

4. true

5. true

6. true

7. true

8. false

9. false

10. true

11. f

12. h

13. d

14. a

15. i

16. e

17. k

18. j

19. g

20. l

21. a

22. d

23. c

24. b

25. b

26. c

27. d

28. a

29. middle

30. Commonwealth

31. restored

32. enclosed

33. the Bible

34. a strong middle class

35. he himself had planned to retire there

36. Example:
They are also individuals described with realistic details.

37. Examples:
the Lilliputians and their Emperor, the Brobdingnagians, the Laputans

38. Example:
He represents a man trying to overcome inner obstacles, trying to save his soul.

1. d

2. i

3. k

4. **a**

5. h

6. b

7. c

8. g

9. j

10. e

11. false

12. false

13. true

14. false

15. true

16. false

17. true

18. true

19. false

20. false

21. d

22. **a**

23. c

24. d

25. c

26. a. climax
    b. resolution or denouement

27. a. flat
    b. round

28. setting

29. composite

30. theme

1. f

2. i

3. k

4. g

5. h

6. c

7. a

8. b

9. d

10. e

11. false

12. true

13. true

14. true

15. false

16. false

17. true

18. false

19. true

20. false

21. b

22. c

23. d

24. b

25. a

26. Oxford movement

27. a. "Ode on a Grecian Urn"
    b. Keats

28. Any order:
    a. larger than life
    b. isolated from society
    c. proud
    d. suffering from some unnamed sin
    or willful, melancholy

29. Any order:
    a. individualism
    b. emotion
    c. mystery
    d. melancholy
    or imagination, simplicity

30. Hopkins

31. Robert Browning

32. Tennyson

1. d

2. f

3. i

4. a

5. j

6. b

7. k

8. c

9. e

10. h

11. true

12. true

13. false

14. false

15. false

16. true

17. false

18. true

19. true

20. true

21. a

22. d

23. c

24. b

25. c

26. Polonius

27. inability to make decisions

28. **alliteration**

29. iambic pentameter

30. Any order:
   a. omniscient
   b. limited omniscient
   c. dramatic
   d. personal

31. Any order:
   a. traditional
   b. transformational
   c. structural

32. Any order:
   a. simile
   b. personification
   c. irony
   or metonymy, metaphor, apostrophe, paradox, synechdoche

33. blank verse

34. Any order:
   a. nature
   b. individuality
   c. personal experience
   d. simplicity
   e. supernatural

35. terza rima